GW00994350

RIDING
RECOLLECTIONS

G. J. Whyte-Melville

RIDING RECOLLECTIONS

G J WHYTE-MELVILLE

Introduced by J. N. P. Watson

**With illustrations by
Hugh Thomson**

• THE •
SPORTSMAN'S
PRESS
LONDON

The publisher gratefully acknowledges the assistance of
University Library, St Andrews, which provided the illustrations
used on the jacket.

© this edition The Sportsman's Press 1985

Originally published in 1875
This edition published in 1985

British Library Cataloguing in Publication Data

Whyte-Melville, G. J.
    Riding recollections.
    1. Horsemanship
    I. Title
    798.2   SF309
    ISBN 0 948253 02 9

Printed and bound in Great Britain by
Redwood Burn Limited, Trowbridge, Wiltshire

The following is a complete list of Whyte-Melville's writings, with the dates of their first publication :—

Digby Grand . . . 1853	Bones and I . . . 1868
General Bounce . . 1854	M. or N. . . . 1869
Kate Coventry . . 1856	Songs and Verses . . 1869
The Arab's Ride to Cairo 1858	Contraband . . . 1870
The Interpreter . . 1858	Sarchedon . . . 1871
Holmby House . . 1860	The True Cross . . 1873
Good for Nothing . . 1861	Satanella . . . 1873
Market Harborough . 1861	Uncle John . . . 1874
Tilbury Nogo . . 1861	Katerfelto . . . 1875
The Queen's Maries . 1862	Sister Louise . . . 1875
The Gladiators . . 1863	Rosine . . . 1875
The Brookes of Bridle-	Riding Recollections . 1875
mere 1864	Roy's Wife . . . 1878
Cerise 1866	Black but Comely . . 1879
The White Rose . . 1868	(posthumous)

INTRODUCTION

"The horse is, of all domestic animals, most susceptible to anything like discomfort or ill-usage", says the author of this classic; "its nervous system, sensitive and highly strung, is capable of daring effort under excitement, but collapses utterly in any new or strange situation . . . From the day you slip a halter over his ears he should be encouraged to look at you like a child for all his little wants and simple pleasures. He should come cantering up from the farthest corner of the paddock when he hears your voice, should ask to have his nose rubbed, his head stroked, his neck patted, with those honest pleading looks which make the confidence of a dumb creature so touching; and before a roller has been put on his back, or a snaffle in his mouth, he should be convinced that everything you do to him is right, and that it is impossible for you, his best friend, to cause him the least uneasiness or harm . . . Even when in fault he should be cautioned rather than reproved".

The 19th century is not an era readily associated, in general, with kindness to animals, nor, in particular, with gentle persuasion for horses. Yet it is difficult to think of any equestrian correspondent in the world who has, to better effect, put high emphasis on care and compassion and the winning of a horse's confidence by love, than Whyte-Melville. Nor does that quality come as a surprise when you know that he was widely regarded as being at once the strongest-willed and most tender, the bravest and most sensitive of men, with a true sympathy for all creatures, whether dumb or of the genus of Adam and Eve. And, as one admirer put it, some years after Whyte-

INTRODUCTION

Melville's death: "Many a story is told even now of his quiet humour and old-fashioned, never-failing courtesy".

Following an Eton education—through which, we are told, "young George acquired a loving reverence for Latin writers, which endured throughout his life and left its stamp on all his writings"—he was commissioned into the Infantry of the Line, transferring after seven years into the Coldstream Guards. He retired in 1839, but rejoined on the outbreak of hostilities with Russia in 1853, serving throughout the Crimean campaign in command of a squadron of Turkish cavalry.

The remainder of Major Whyte-Melville's life was largely divided between hunting in the winter, golf on the links of his native St Andrews in the summer, historical research and—writing. A born story-teller, lucid composer of prose and untiring worker, he produced no fewer than 28 books, mostly novels, in 26 years. His first love was the hunting-field. Only two 19th-century scribes, "Nimrod" and "Brooksby", rendered such a sense of excitement to that arena as he did, and probably none gave it such a readable air of romance.

When he chose a hunting-box in the parish of Tetbury, in Gloucestershire, one of his friends criticised it as being "too close to the churchyard", to which Whyte-Melville replied: "perhaps it is for some tastes; but the closer the better for a hunting man; they will not have so far to carry him". The words were tragically prophetic. Not long after that, when he was out with the VWH on the 5th of December, 1878, anticipating hounds breaking covert, he galloped along a hedgerow to gain a head-start. His favourite hunter Shah, crossed his legs, fell and threw him. Whyte-Melville was found stone dead. He was buried in the Tetbury graveyard, aged 57.

Riding Recollections, which had been published three years earlier, is a somewhat misleading title. It is written rather as an uncle

INTRODUCTION

might write to a favourite, if not always very attentive, nephew. "This is how you should make and break a horse", the book advises in so many words; "this is how you should choose a horse, saddle, bit and bridle him; how you should cope with a cold, a hot, a veteran, a green horse; how you should judge between an English and an Irish offer; how you should follow hounds; how you should put your hunter at a bullfinch, an oxer, a five-bar gate, an Irish double; this is when to be bold, when to be cautious; this is how to care for your horse at the end of the day . . .".

Major Whyte-Melville does, however, sometimes make it all sound a little too easy. Listen to this! "The great art of horsemanship . . . is to find out what the animal requires of us, and to meet its wishes, even its prejudices, half-way. Cool with the rash, and daring with the cautious, it is wise to retain the semblance, at least of a self-possession superior to casualties, and equal to any emergency, from a refusal to a fall . . ." That he himself owned that rare "self-possession" is certain. But how many of the tyros he addresses, we wonder, ever acquired it?

In Whyte-Melville's Britain showjumping and eventing were non-existent, *haute ecole* very rare, polo in its infancy. Hunting was the only serious sporting equestrianism the Englishman knew. A man was largely judged "good" horseman or "bad" horseman by his skill or ineptitude in the hunting-field and Whyte-Melville is famous today for nothing if not his confession: "I freely admit that the best of my fun I owe it to horse and hound". Most of his comments are therefore related to that sphere, but to a hunting-field very different from the one we know today, a much less intensively farmed, wilder, freer countryside in which foxhunters rode more or less where they liked, taking their own line.

That is not to say, however, that the hunting-field does not remain

INTRODUCTION

the best general academy for the budding equestrian. The late
Col. Guy Cubitt, founder of the Pony Club, said to me, a few months
before he died: "All this competitive stuff the children go in for
nowadays—its the best thing in the world to teach them selfishness,
bad manners and poor horsemanship. When I started the Pony
Club my aim was that young people should be taught primarily
through the fraternity of the hunting-field. Most of that seems to
have gone now . . ." Had George Whyte-Melville been a mid-20th
century man how strongly he would have sympathised with Guy
Cubitt!

But *Riding Recollections* is not a children's book, it is a sophisticated
treatise, and a very entertaining one, too, in which the ruling theme,
reflecting the fine character of the man, is: "Be grateful to your horses
honour them, love them, and they will give the same in return".

J. N. P. WATSON

Country Life,
King's Reach Tower,
Stamford St.,
Blackfriars,
London.

x

A RUM ONE TO FOLLOW, A BAD ONE
TO BEAT

COME, I'll give you the health of a man we all know,
    A man we all swear by, a friend of our own ;
With the hounds running hardest, he's safest to go,
    And he's always in front, and he's often alone.
A rider unequalled—a sportsman complete,
A rum one to follow, a bad one to beat.

As he sits in the saddle, a baby could tell
    He can hustle a sticker, a flyer can spare ;
He has science, and nerve, and decision as well,
    He knows where he's going and means to be there.
The first day I saw him they said at the meet,
" That's a rum one to follow, a bad one to beat."

We threw off at the Castle, we found in the holt,
    Like wildfire the beauties went streaming away ;
From the rest of the field he came out like a bolt,
    And he tackled to work like a schoolboy to play,
As he rammed down his hat, and got home in his seat,
This rum one to follow, this bad one to beat.

'Twas a caution, I vow, but to see the man ride !
    O'er the rough and the smooth he went sailing along ;
And what Providence sent him, he took in his stride,
    Though the ditches were deep, and the fences were strong.
Thinks I, " If he leads me I'm in for a treat,
With this rum one to follow, this bad one to beat!"

Ere they'd run for a mile, there was room in the front,
  Such a scatter and squander you never did see!
And I honestly own I'd been out of the hunt,
  But the broad of his back was the beacon for me.
So I kept him in sight, and was proud of the feat,
This rum one to follow, this bad one to beat!

Till we came to a rasper as black as your hat,
  You couldn't see over—you couldn't see through;
So he made for the gate, knowing what he was at,
  And the chain being round it, why—over he flew!
While I swore a round oath that I needn't repeat,
At this rum one to follow, this bad one to beat.

For a place I liked better I hastened to seek,
  But the place I liked better I sought for in vain;
And I honestly own, if the truth I must speak,
  That I never caught sight of my leader again.
But I thought, " I'd give something to have his receipt,
This rum one to follow, this bad one to beat."

They told me that night he went best through the run,
  They said that he hung up a dozen to dry,
When a brook in the bottom stopped most of their fun,
  But I know that I never went near it, not I.
For I found it a fruitless attempt to compete
With this rum one to follow, this bad one to beat.

So we'll fill him a bumper as deep as you please,
  And we'll give him a cheer; for, deny it who can,
When the country is roughest he's most at his ease;
  When the run is severest, he rides like a man.
And the pace cannot stop, nor the fences defeat,
This rum one to follow, this bad one to beat.

G. J. WHYTE-MELVILLE

CONTENTS

LIST OF ILLUSTRATIONS

AUTHOR'S PREFACE

AS in the choice of a horse and a wife a man must please himself, ignoring the opinion and advice of friends, so in the governing of each it is unwise to follow out any fixed system of discipline. Much depends on temper, education, mutual understanding, and surrounding circumstances. Courage must not be heated to recklessness, caution should be implied rather than exhibited, and confidence is simply a question of time and place. It is as difficult to explain by precept or demonstrate by example how force, balance, and persuasion ought to be combined in horsemanship, as to teach the art of floating in the water or swimming on the back. Practice in either case alone makes perfect, and he is the most apt pupil who brings to his lesson a good opinion of his own powers and implicit reliance on that which carries him. Trust the element or the animal and you ride aloft superior to

B   xvii

danger; but with misgiving comes confusion, effort, breathlessness, possibly collapse and defeat. Morally and physically, there is no creature so nervous as a man out of his depth.

In offering the following pages to the public, the writer begs emphatically to disclaim any intention of laying down the law on such a subject as horsemanship. Every man who wears spurs believes himself more or less an adept in the art of riding; and it would be the height of presumption for one who has studied that art as a pleasure and not a profession to dictate for the ignorant, or enter the lists of argument with the wise. All he can lay claim to is a certain amount of experience, the result of many happy hours spent with the noble animal under him, of some uncomfortable minutes when mutual indiscretion has caused that position to be reversed.

If the few hints he can offer should prove serviceable to the beginner he will feel amply rewarded, and will only ask to be kindly remembered hereafter in the hour of triumph when the tyro of a riding-school has become the pride of a hunting-field—judicious, cool, daring, and skilful, light of hand, firm of seat, thoroughly at home in the saddle, a very Centaur—

> " Encorpsed and demi-natured
> With the brave beast."

RIDING
RECOLLECTIONS

RIDING RECOLLECTIONS

CHAPTER I

KINDNESS

IN our dealings with the brute creation, it cannot be too much insisted on that mutual confidence is only to be established by mutual goodwill. The perceptions of the beast must be raised to their highest standard, and there is no such enemy to intelligence as fear. Reward should be as the daily food it eats, punishment as the medicine administered on rare occasions, unwillingly, and but when absolute necessity demands. The horse is of all domestic animals most susceptible to anything like discomfort or ill-usage. Its nervous system, sensitive and highly strung, is capable of daring effort under excitement, but collapses utterly in any new and strange situation, as if paralysed by apprehensions of the unknown.

Can anything be more helpless than the young horse you take out hunting the first time he finds himself in a bog? Compare his frantic struggles and sudden prostration with the discreet conduct of an Exmoor pony in the same predicament. The one terrified by unaccustomed danger, and relying instinctively on the speed that seems his natural refuge, plunges wildly forward, sinks to his girths, his shoulders, finally unseats his rider, and settles down, without further exertion, in the stupid apathy of despair. The other, born and bred in the wild west country, picking its scanty keep from a foal off the treacherous surface of a Devonshire moor, either refuses altogether to trust the quagmire, or shortens its stride, collects its energies, chooses the soundest tufts that afford foothold, and failing these, flaps its way out on its side, to scramble into safety with scarce a quiver or a snort. It has been there before! Herein lies the whole secret.

Some day your young one will be as calm, as wise, as tractable. Alas! that when his discretion has reached its prime his legs begin to fail! Therefore cultivate his intellect—I use the word advisedly—even before you enter on the development of his physical powers. Nature and good keep will provide for these, but to make him man's willing friend and partner you must give him the advantage of man's company and man's instruction. From the day you slip a halter over his ears he should be encouraged to look to you, like a child, for all his little wants and simple pleasures. He should come cantering up from the farthest corner of the paddock when he hears your voice, should ask to have his nose rubbed, his head stroked, his neck patted, with those honest, pleading looks which make the confidence of a dumb creature so touching; and before a roller has been put on his back, or a snaffle in his mouth, he should be convinced that everything you do to him is right, and that it is impossible for *you*, his best friend, to cause him the least uneasiness or harm.

I once owned a mare that would push her nose into my pockets in search of bread and sugar, would lick my face and hands like a dog, or suffer me to cling to any part of her limbs and body while she stood perfectly motionless. On one occasion, when I hung in the stirrup after a fall, she never stirred on rising, till by a succession of laborious and ludicrous efforts I could swing myself back into the saddle, with my foot still fast, though hounds were running hard and she loved hunting dearly in her heart. As a friend remarked at the time, "The little mare seems very fond of you, or there might have been a bother!"

Now this affection was but the result of petting, sugar, kind and encouraging words, particularly at her fences, and a rigid abstinence from abuse of the bridle and the spur. I shall presently have something to say about both these instruments, but I may remark in the meantime that many more horses than people suppose will cross a country safely with a loose rein. The late Colonel William Greenwood, one of the finest riders in the world, might be seen out hunting with a single curb-bridle, such as is called "a hard-and-sharp" and commonly used only in the streets of London or the Park. The present Lord Spencer, of whom it is enough to say that he hunts one pack of his own hounds in Northamptonshire, and is always *in the same field with them*, never seems to have a horse pull, or until it is tired, even lean on his hand. I have watched both these gentlemen intently to learn their secret, but I regret to say without avail.

This, however, is not the present question. Long before a bridle is fitted on the colt's head he should have so thoroughly learned the habit of obedience, that it has become a second instinct, and to do what is required of him seems as natural as to eat when he is hungry or lie down when he wants to sleep.

This result is to be attained in a longer or shorter time, according to different tempers, but the first and most important step is surely gained when we have succeeded in winning that affection which nurses and children call "cupboard love." Like many amiable characters on two legs, the quadruped is shy of acquaintances but genial with friends. Make him understand that you are his best and wisest, that all you do conduces to his comfort and happiness, be careful at first not to deceive or disappoint him, and you will find his reasoning powers quite strong enough to grasp the relations of cause and effect.

In a month or six weeks he will come to your call, and follow you about like a dog. Soon he will let you lift his feet, handle him all over, pull his tail, and lean your weight on any part of his body, without alarm or resentment. When thoroughly familiar with your face, your voice, and the motions of your limbs, you may back him with perfect safety, and he will move as soberly under you in any place to which he is accustomed as the oldest horse in your stable.

Do not forget, however, that education should be gradual as moon-rise, perceptible, not in progress, but result. I recollect one morning riding to covert with a Dorsetshire farmer whose horses, bred at home, were celebrated as timber-jumpers even in that most timber-jumping of countries. I asked him how they arrived at this proficiency without breaking somebody's neck, and he imparted his plan.

The colt, it seemed, ran loose from a yearling in the owner's straw-yard, but fed in a lofty out-house, across the door of which was placed a single tough ashen bar that would not break under a bullock. This was laid on the ground till the young one had grown thoroughly accustomed to it, and then raised very gradually to such a height as was less trouble to jump than clamber over. At three feet the two-year-old thought no more of the obstacle than a girl does of her skipping-rope. After that, it was heightened an inch every week, and it needs no ready reckoner to tell us at the end of six months how formidable a leap the animal voluntarily negotiated three times a day.

"It's never put no higher," continued my informant; "I'm an old man now, and that's good enough for me."

I should think it was! A horse that can leap five feet of timber in cold blood is not likely to be pounded, while still unblown, in any part of England I have yet seen.

Now the Dorsetshire farmer's system was sound, and based on common sense. As you bend the twig so grows the tree, therefore prepare your pupil from the first for the purpose you intend him to serve hereafter. An Arab foal, as we know, brought up in the Bedouin's tent, like another child, among the Bedouin's children, is the most docile of its kind, and I cannot but think that if he lived in our houses and we took as much notice of him, the horse would prove quite as sagacious as the dog; but we must never forget that to harshness or intimidation he is the most sensitive of creatures, and even when in fault should be rather cautioned than reproved.

An ounce of illustration is worth a pound of argument, and the following example best conveys the spirit in which our brave and willing servant should be treated by his lord.

Many years ago, when he hunted the Cottesmore country, Sir Richard Sutton's hounds had been running hard from Glooston Wood along the valley under Cranehoe by Slawston to Holt. After thirty minutes or so over this beautiful, but exceedingly stiff line, their heads went up, and they came to a check, possibly from their own dash and eagerness, certainly, at that pace and amongst those fences, *not from being overridden*.

"Turn 'em, Ben!" exclaimed Sir Richard, with a dirty coat, and Hotspur in a lather, but determined not to lose a moment in getting after his fox.

"Yes, Sir Richard," answered Morgan, running his horse without a moment's hesitation at a flight of double-posts and rails, with a ditch in the middle and one on each side! The good grey, having gone in front from the find, was perhaps a little blown, and dropping his hind legs in the farthest ditch, rolled very handsomely into the next field.

"It's not *your* fault, old man!" said Ben, patting his favourite on the neck as they rose together in mutual goodwill, adding in the same breath, while he leapt to the saddle, and Tranby acknowledged the line—" Forrard on, Sir Richard! —Hoic together, hoic! You'll have him directly, my beauties! He's a Quorn fox, and he'll do you good!"

I had always considered Ben Morgan an unusually fine rider. For the first time, I began to understand *why* his horse never failed to carry him so willingly and so well.

I do not remember whether Dick Webster was out with us that day, but I am sure if he was he has not forgotten it, and I mention him as another example of daring horsemanship combined with an imperturbable good humour, almost verging on buffoonery, which seems to accept the most dangerous falls as enhancing the fun afforded by a delightful game of romps. His annual exhibition of prowess at the Islington horse show has made his shrewd, comical face so familiar to the public that his name, without further comment, is enough to recall the presence and bearing of the man—his quips and cranks and merry jests, his shrill whistle and ready smile, his strong seat and light, skilful hand, but above all his untiring patience and unfailing kindness with the most restive and refractory of pupils. Dick, like many other good fellows, is not so young as he was, but he will probably be an unequalled rider at eighty, and I am quite sure that if he lives to the age of Methuselah, the extreme of senile irritability will never provoke him to lose his temper with a horse.

Presence of mind under difficulties is the one quality that in riding makes all the difference between getting off with a scramble and going down with a fall. If unvaried kindness has taught your horse to place confidence in his rider, he will have his wits about him, and provide for *your* safety as for his own. When left to himself, and not flurried by the fear of punishment, even an inexperienced hunter makes surprising efforts to keep on his legs, and it is not too much to say that while his wind lasts, the veteran is almost as difficult to catch tripping as a cat. I have known horses drop their hind legs on places scarcely affording foothold for a goat, but in all such feats they have been ridden by a lover of the animal, who trusts it implicitly, and rules by kindness rather than fear.

I will not deny that there are cases in which the *suaviter in modo* must be supplemented by the *fortiter in re*. Still the insubordination of ignorance is never wholly inexcusable, and great discretion must be used in repressing even the most violent of outbreaks. If severity is absolutely required, be sure to temper justice with mercy, remembering that, in brute natures at least, the more you spare the rod, the less you spoil the child!

CHAPTER II

COERCION

I RECOLLECT, in years gone by, an old and pleasant comrade used to declare that "to be in a rage was almost as contemptible as to be in a funk!" Doubtless the passion of anger, though less despised than that of fear, is so far derogatory to the dignity of man that it deprives him temporarily of reason, the very quality which confers sovereignty over the brute. When a magician is without his talisman the slaves he used to rule will do his bidding no longer. When we say of such a one that he has "lost his head," we no more expect him to steer a judicious course than a ship that has lost her rudder. Both are the prey of circumstances—at the mercy of winds and waves. Therefore, however hard you are compelled to hit, be sure to keep your temper. Strike in perfect good-humour, and in the right place. Many people cannot encounter resistance of any kind without anger, even a difference of opinion in conversation is sufficient to rouse their

COERCION

bile ; but such are seldom winners in argument or
in fight. Let them also leave education alone.
Nature never meant them to teach the young
idea how to shoot or hunt, or do anything else !

It is the cold-blooded and sagacious wrestler
who takes the prize, the calm and imperturbable
player who wins the game. In all struggles for
supremacy, excitement only produces flurry, and
flurry means defeat.

Who ever saw Mr. Anstruther Thompson in a
passion, though, like every other huntsman and
master of hounds, he must often have found his
temper sorely tried ? And yet, when punishment
is absolutely necessary to extort obedience from
the equine rebel, no man can administer it more
severely, either from the saddle or the box. But
whether double-thonging a restive wheeler, or
"having it out" with a resolute buck-jumper, the
operation is performed with the same pleasant
smile, and when one of the adversaries preserves
calmness and common sense, the fight is soon
over, and the victory gained.

It is not every man, however, who possesses
this gentleman's iron nerve and powerful frame.
For most of us, it is well to remember, before
engaging in such contests, that defeat is absolute
ruin. We must be prepared to fight it out to the
bitter end, and if we are not sure of our own
firmness, either mental or physical, it is well to

temporise, and try to win by diplomacy the terms we dare not wrest by force. If the latter alternative must needs be accepted, in this as in most stand-up fights, it will be found that the first blow is half the battle. The rider should take his horse short by the head and let him have two or three stingers with a cutting whip—not more —particularly, if on a thoroughbred one, as low down the flanks as can be reached, administered without warning, and in quick succession, sitting back as prepared for the plunge into the air that will inevitably follow, keeping his horse's head well up the while to prevent buck-jumping. He should then turn the animal round and round half a dozen times, till it is confused, and start it off at a speed in any direction where there is room for a gallop. Blown, startled, and intimidated, he will in all probability find his pupil perfectly amenable to reason when he pulls up, and should then coax and soothe him into an equable frame of mind once more. Such, however, is an extreme case. It is far better to avoid the *ultima ratio*. In equitation, as in matrimony, there should never arise *the first quarrel*. Obedience, in horses, ought to be a matter of habit, contracted so imperceptibly that its acquirement can scarcely be called a lesson.

This is why the hunting-field is such a good school for leaping. Horses of every kind are prompted by some unaccountable impulse to follow a pack of hounds, and the beginner finds himself voluntarily performing feats of activity and daring, in accordance with the will of his rider, which no coercion from the latter would have induced him to attempt. Flushed with success, and if fortunate enough to escape a fall, confident in his lately-discovered powers, he finds a new pleasure in their exercise, and, most precious of qualities in a hunter, grows "fond of jumping."

The same result is to be attained at home, but is far more gradual, requiring the exercise of much care, patience, and perseverance.

Nevertheless, when we consider the inconvenience created by the vagaries of young horses in the hunting-field, to hounds, sportsmen, ladies, pedestrians, and their own riders, we must admit that the Irish system is best, and that a colt, to use the favourite expression, should have been trained into "an accomplished lepper," before he is asked to carry a sportsman through a run.

Mr. Rarey, no doubt, thoroughly understood the nature of the animal with which he had to deal. His system was but a convenient application of our principle, viz., Judicious coercion, so employed that the brute obeys the man without knowing why. When forced to the earth, and compelled to remain there, apparently by the mere volition of a creature so much smaller and feebler than itself, it seemed to acknowledge some mysterious and overmastering power such as the disciples of Mesmer profess to exercise on their believers, and this, in truth, is the whole secret of man's dominion over the beasts of the field. It is founded, to speak practically, on reason in both, the larger share being apportioned to the weaker frame. If by terror or resentment, the result of injudicious severity, that reason becomes obscured in the stronger animal, we have a maniac to deal with, possessing the strength of ten human beings, over whom we have lost our only shadow of control! Where is our supremacy then? It existed but in the imagination of the beast, for which, so long as it never tried to break the bond, a silken thread was as strong as an iron chain.

Perhaps this is the theory of all government, but with the conduct and coercion of mankind we have at present nothing to do.

There is a peculiarity in horses that none who spend much time in the saddle can have failed to notice. It is the readiness with which all accommodate themselves to a rider who succeeds in subjugating *one*. Some men possess a faculty, impossible to explain, of establishing a good understanding from the moment they place themselves in the saddle. It can hardly be called hand, for I have seen consummate horsemen, notably Mr. Lovell, of the New Forest, who have lost an arm; nor seat, or how could Colonel Fraser, late of the 11th Hussars, be one of the best heavy-weights over such a country as Meath, with a broken and contracted thigh? Certainly not nerve, for there are few fields too scanty to furnish examples of men who possess every quality of horsemanship except daring. What is it, then? I cannot tell, but if you are fortunate enough to possess it, whether you weigh ten stone or twenty, you will be able to mount yourself fifty pounds cheaper than anybody else in the market! Be it an impulse of nature, or a result of education, there is a tendency in every horse to make vigorous efforts at the shortest notice in obedience to the inclination of a rider's body or the pressure of his limbs. Such indications are of the utmost service in an emergency, and to offer them at the happy moment is a crucial test of horsemanship. Thus races are "snatched out of the fire," as it is termed, by riding; and this is the quality that, where judgment, patience, and knowledge of pace are equal, renders one jockey superior to the rest. It enables a proficient also to clear those large fences that, in our grazing districts especially, appear impracticable to the uninitiated, as if the horse borrowed muscular energy, no less than mental courage, from the resolution of his rider. On the racecourse and in the hunting - field, Custance, the well-known jockey, possesses this quality in the highest degree. The same determined strength in the saddle, that had done him such good service amongst the bullfinches and "oxers"of his native Rutland, applied at the happy moment, secured on a great occasion his celebrated victory with King Lud.

There are two kinds of hunters that require coercion in following hounds, and he is indeed a master of his art who feels equally at home on each. The one must be *steered*, the other *smuggled* over a country. As he is never comfortable but in front, we will take the rash horse first.

Let us suppose you have not ridden him before, that you like his appearance, his action, all his qualities except his boundless ambition, that you are in a practicable country, as seems only fair, and about to draw a covert affording every prospect of a run. Before you put your foot in the stirrup be sure to examine his bit— not one groom in a hundred knows how to bridle a horse properly—and remember that on the fitting of this important article depends your success, your enjoyment, perhaps your safety, during the day. Horses, like servants, will never let their master be happy if they are un

18

comfortable themselves. See that your headstall is long enough, so that the pressure may lie on the bars of the horse's mouth and not crumple up the corners of his lips, like a gag. The curb-chain will probably be too tight, also the throat-lash; if so, loosen both, and with your own hands; it is a pleasant way of making acquaintance, and may perhaps prepossess him in your favour. If he wears a nose-band it will be time enough to take it off when you find he shows impatience of the restriction by shaking his head, changing his leg frequently, or reaching unjustifiably at the rein.

I am prejudiced against the nose-band. I frankly admit a man in a minority of one *must* be wrong, but I never rode a horse in my life that, to my own feeling, did not go more comfortably when I took it off.

Look also to your girths. For a fractious temper they are very irritating when drawn too tight, while with good shape and a breastplate, there is little danger of their not being tight enough. When these preliminaries have been carefully gone through mount nimbly to the saddle, and take the first opportunity of feeling your new friend's mouth and paces in trot, canter, and gallop. Here, too, though in general it should be avoided for many reasons, social, agricultural, and personal, a little "larking" is not wholly inexcusable. It will promote cordiality between man and beast. The latter, as we are considering him, is sure to be fond of jumping, and to ride him over a fence or two away from other horses in cold blood will create in his mind the very desirable impression that you are of a daring spirit, determined to be in front.

Take him, however, up to his leap as slow as he will permit—if possible at a trot. Even should he break into a canter and become impetuous at last, there is no space for a violent rush in three strides, during which you must hold him in a firm, equable grasp. As he leaves the ground give him his head, he cannot have "too much rope," till he lands again, when, as soon as possible, you should pull him back to a trot, handling him delicately, soothing him with voice and gesture, treating the whole affair as the simplest matter of course. Do not bring him again over the same place, rather take him on for two or three fields in a line parallel to the hounds. By the time they are put into covert you will have established a mutual understanding, and found out how much you *dislike* one another at the worst! It is well now to avoid the crowd, but beware of taking up a position by yourself where you may head the fox! No man can ride in good-humour under a sense of guilt, and you *must* be good-humoured with such a mount as you have under you to-day.

COERCION

Exhaust, therefore, all your knowledge of woodcraft to get away on good terms with the hounds. The wildest romp in a rush of horses is often perfectly temperate and amenable when called on to cut out the work. Should you, by ill luck, find yourself behind others in the first field, avoid, if possible, following any one of them over the first fence. Even though it be somewhat black and forbidding, choose a fresh place ; so free a horse as yours will jump the more carefully that his attention is not distracted by a leader, and there is the further consideration, based on common humanity, that your leader might fall when too late for you to stop. No man is in so false a position as he who rides over a friend in the hunting - field, except the friend !

Take your own line. If you be not afraid to gallop and the hounds *run on*, you will probably find it plain sailing till they check. Should a brook laugh in your face, of no unreasonable dimensions, you may charge it with confidence ; a rash horse usually jumps width, and there will be plenty of "room to ride" on the far side. It takes but a few feet of water to decimate a field. I may here observe that, if, as they cross, you see the hounds leap at it, even though they fall short, you may be sure the distance from bank to bank is within the compass of a hunter's stride.

RIDING RECOLLECTIONS

At timber, I would not have you quite so confident. When, as in Leicestershire, it is set fairly in line with the fence and there is a good take - off, your horse, however impetuous, may leap it with impunity in his stroke, but should the ground be poached by cattle, or dip as you come to it, beware of too great hurry. The feat ought then to be accomplished calmly and collectedly at a trot, the horse taking his time, so to speak, from the motions of his rider, and jumping, as it is called, "to his hand." Now when man and horse are at variance on so important a matter as pace, the one is almost sure to interfere at the wrong moment, the other to take off too soon or get too close under his leap ; in either case the animal is more likely to rise at a fence than a rail, and if unsuccessful in clearing it a binder is less dangerous to flirt with than a bar. Lord Wilton seems to me to ride at timber a turn slower than usual, Lord Grey a turn faster. Whether father and son differ in theory I am unable to say, I can only affirm that both are undeniable in practice. Mr. Fellowes of Shottisham, perhaps the best of his day, and Mr. Gilmour, *facile princeps*, almost walk up to this kind of leap ; Colonel, now General Pearson, known for so many seasons as "the flying Captain," charges it like a squadron of Sikh cavalry ; Captain Arthur Smith pulls back to a

22

COERCION

trot; Lord Carington scarcely shortens the stride of his gallop. Who shall decide between such professors? Much depends on circumstances, more perhaps on horses. Assheton Smith used to throw the reins on a hunter's neck when rising at a gate, and say, "Take care of yourself, you brute!"—whereas the celebrated Lord Jersey, who gave me this information of his old friend's style, held his own bridle in a vice at such emergencies, and both usually got safe over! Perhaps the logical deduction from these conflicting examples should be not to jump timber at all!

But the rash horse is by this time getting tired, and now, if you would avoid a casualty, you must temper valour with discretion, and ride him as skilfully as you *can*.

He has probably carried you well and pleasantly during the few happy moments that intervened between freshness and fatigue; now he is beginning to pull again, but in a more set and determined manner than at first. He does not collect himself so readily, and wants to go faster than ever at his fences, if you would let him. This careless, rushing style threatens a downfall, and to counteract it will require the exercise of your utmost skill. Carry his head for him, since he seems to require it, and endeavour, by main force if necessary, to bring him to his leaps with his hind legs under him. Half-beaten horses measure distance with great accuracy, and "lob" over very large places, when properly ridden. If, notwithstanding all your precautions, he persists in going on his shoulders, blundering through his places, and labouring across ridge and furrow like a boat in a heavy sea, take advantage of the first lane you find, and voting the run nearly over, make up your mind to view the rest of it in safety from the hard road!

Ride the same horse again at the first opportunity, and, if sound enough to come out in his turn, a month's open weather will probably make him a very pleasant mount.

The "slug," a thoroughbred one, we will say, with capital hind ribs, lop ears, and a lazy eye, must be managed on a very different system from the foregoing. You need not be so particular about his bridle, for the coercion in this case is of impulsion rather than restraint, but I would advise you to select a useful cutting-whip, stiff and strong enough to push a gate. Not that you must use it freely—one or two "reminders" at the right moment, and an occasional flourish, ought to carry you through the day. Be sure, too, that you strike underhanded, and not in front of your own body, lest you take his eye off at the critical moment when your horse is measuring his leap. The best riders prefer such an instrument to the spurs, as a stimulant to increased pace and momentary exertion.

You will have little trouble with this kind of hunter while hounds are drawing. He will seem only too happy to stand still, and you may sit amongst your friends in the middle ride, smoking, joking, and holding forth to your heart's content. But, like the fox, you will find your troubles begin with the cheering holloa of "Gone away!"

On your present mount, instead of avoiding the crowd, I should advise you to keep in the very midst of the torrent that, pent up in covert, rushes down the main ride to choke a narrow handgate, and overflow the adjoining field. Emerging from the jaws of their inconvenient egress, they will scatter, like a row of beads when the string breaks, and while the majority incline to right or left, regardless of the line of chase as compared with that of safety, some half-dozen are sure to single themselves out, and ride straight after the hounds.

Select one of these, a determined horseman, whom you know to be mounted on an experienced hunter; give him *plenty of room*—fifty yards at least—and ride his line, nothing doubting, fence for fence, till your horse's blood is up, and your own too. I cannot enough insist on a jealous care of your leader's safety, and a little consideration for his prejudices. The boldest sportsmen are exceedingly touchy about being ridden over, and not without reason. There is something unpleasantly suggestive in the bit and teeth and tongue of an open mouth at your ear; while your own horse, quivering high in air, makes the discovery that he has not allowed margin enough for the yawner under his nose! It is little less inexcusable to pick a man's pocket than to ride in it; and no apology can exonerate so flagrant an assault as to land on him when down. Reflect, also, that a hunter, after the effort to clear his fence, often loses foothold, particularly over ridge and furrow, in the second or third stride, and falls at the very moment a follower would suppose he was safe over. Therefore, do not begin for yourself till your leader is twenty yards into the next field, when you may harden your heart, set your muscles, and give your horse to understand, by seat and manner, that it must be in, through, or over.

Beware, however, of hurrying him off his legs. Ride him resolutely, indeed, but in a short, contracted stride; slower in proportion to the unwillingness he betrays, so as to hold him in a vice, and squeeze him up to the brink of his task, when, forbidden to turn from it, he will probably make his effort in self-defence, and take you somehow to the other side. Not one hunter in a hundred can jump in good form when going at

Choking a narrow handgate

speed; it is the perfection of equine prowess, resulting from great quickness and the confidence of much experience. An arrant refuser usually puts on the steam of his own accord, like a confirmed rusher, and wheels to right or left at the last moment, with an activity that, displayed in a better cause, would be beyond praise. The rider, too, has more command of his horse, when forced up to the bit in a slow canter than at any other pace.

Thoroughbred horses, until their education is complete, are apt to get very close to their fences, preferring, as it would seem, to go into them on this side rather than the other. It is not a style that inspires confidence; yet these crafty, careful creatures are safer than they seem, and from jumping in a collected form, with their hind legs under them, extricate themselves with surprising address from difficulties that, after a little more tuition, they will never be in. They are really less afraid of their fences, and consequently less flurried, than the wilful, impetuous brute that loses its equanimity from the moment it catches sight of an obstacle, and miscalculating its distance, in sheer nervousness—most fatal error of all— takes off too soon.

I will now suppose that in the wake of your pilot you have negotiated two or three fences with some expenditure of nerve and temper, but without a refusal or a fall. The cutting-whip has been applied, and the result, perhaps, was disappointing, for it is an uncertain remedy, though, in my opinion, preferable to the spur. Your horse has shown great leaping powers in the distances he has covered without the momentum of speed, and has doubled an on-and-off with a precision not excelled by your leader himself. If he would but jump in his stride, you feel you have a hunter under you. Should the country be favourable, now is the time to teach him this accomplishment, while his limbs are supple and his spirit roused. If he seems willing to face them, let him take his fences in his own way; do not force or hurry him, but keep fast hold of his head without varying the pressure of hand or limb by a hairsbreadth; the least uncertainty of finger or inequality of seat will spoil it all. Should the ditch be towards him, he will jump from a stand, or nearly so, but, to your surprise, will land safe in the next field. If it is on the far side, he will show more confidence, and will perhaps swing over the whole with something of an effort in his canter. A foot or two of extra width may cause him to drop a hind leg, or even bring him on his nose; so much the better! no admonition of yours would have proved as effectual a warning; he will take good care to cover distance enough next time. Dispense with your leader now, if you are pretty close to the hounds, for your horse is gathering confidence with every stride. He can gallop, of course, and is good through dirt; it is also understood that he is fit to go; there are not many in a season, but let us suppose you have dropped into a run; if he carries you well to the finish, he will be a hunter from to-day.

After some five-and-twenty minutes, you will find him going with more dash and freedom, as his neighbours begin to tire. You may now ride him at timber without scruple, when not too high, but avoid a rail that looks as if it would break. To find out he may tamper with such an obstacle is the most dangerous discovery a hunter can make. You should send him at it pretty quick, lest he get too near to rise, and refuse at the last moment. He may not do it in the best of form, but whether he chances it in his gallop, or bucks over like a deer, or hoists himself sideways all in a heap, with his tail against your hat, at this kind of fence this kind of horse is most unlikely to fall.

The same may be said of a brook. If he is within a fair distance of the hounds, and you see by the expression of his ears and crest that he is watching them with ardent interest, ride him boldly at water should it be necessary. It is quite possible he may jump it in his stride from bank to bank, without a moment's hesitation. It is equally possible he may stop short on the bank, with lowered head and crouching quarters as if prepared to drink, or dive, or decline. He will do none of these. Sit still, give him his head, keep close in to your saddle, not moving so much as an eyelash, and it is more than probable that he will jump the stream standing, and reach the other side, with a scramble and a flounder at the worst!

If he should drop his hind legs, *shoot* yourself off over his shoulders in an instant, with a fast hold of the bridle, at which tug hard, even though you may not have regained your legs. A very slight help now will enable him to extricate himself, but if he is allowed to subside into the gulf, it may take a team of cart horses to drag him out.

When in the saddle again give him a timely pull; after the struggle you will be delighted with each other, and have every prospect of going on triumphantly to the end.

I have here endeavoured to describe the different methods of coercion by which two opposite natures may be induced to exert themselves on our behalf in the chase. Every horse inclines, more or less, to one or other extreme I have cited as an example. A perfect hunter has preserved the good qualities of each without the faults, but how many perfect hunters do any of us ride in our lives ? The chestnut is as fast as the wind, stout and honest, a safe and gallant fencer, but too light a mouth makes him difficult to handle at blind and cramped places ; the bay can leap like a deer, and climb like a goat, invincible at doubles, and unrivalled at rails, but, as bold Lord Cardigan said of an equally accomplished animal, "it takes him a long time to get from one bit of timber to another!" While the brown, even faster than the chestnut, even safer than the bay, would be the best, as he is the pleasantest hunter in the world —only nothing will induce him to go near a brook!

It is only by exertion of a skill that is the embodiment of thought in action, by application of a science founded on reason, experience, and analogy, that we can approach perfection in our noble four-footed friend. Common-sense will do much, kindness more, coercion very little, yet we are not to forget that man is the master ; that the hand, however light, must be strong, the heel, however lively, must be resolute ; and that when persuasion, best of all inducements, seems to fail, we must not shrink from the timely application of force.

CHAPTER III

THE USE OF THE BRIDLE

THE late Mr. Maxse, celebrated some fifty years ago for a fineness of hand that enabled him to cross Leicestershire with fewer falls than any other sportsman of fifteen stone who rode equally straight, used to profess much comical impatience with the insensibility of his servants to this useful quality. He was once seen explaining what he meant to his coachman with a silk handkerchief passed round a post.

"Pull at it!" said the master. "Does it pull at you?"

"Yes, sir," answered the servant, grinning.

"Slack it off, then. Does it pull at you now?"

"No, sir."

"Well, then, you double-distilled fool, can't you see that your horses are like that post? If you don't pull at *them* they won't pull at *you*!"

Now it seems to me that in riding, and driving also, what we want to teach our horses is, that when we pull at them they are *not* to pull at us,

32

THE USE OF THE BRIDLE

and this understanding is only to be attained by a delicacy of touch, a harmony of intention, and a give-and-take concord, that for lack of a better we express by the term "hand." Like the fingering of a pianoforte, this desirable quality seems rather a gift than an acquirement, and its rarity has no doubt given rise to the multiplicity of inventions with which man's ingenuity endeavours to supply the want of manual skill.

It was the theory of a celebrated Yorkshire sportsman, the well-known Mr. Fairfax, that "Every horse is a hunter if you don't throw him down with the bridle!" and I have always understood his style of riding was in perfect accordance with this daring profession of faith. The instrument, however, though no doubt producing ten falls, where it prevents one, is in so far a necessary evil, that we are helpless without it, and when skilfully used in conjunction with legs, knees, and body by a consummate horseman, would seem to convey the man's intentions to the beast through some subtle agency, mysterious and almost rapid as thought. It is impossible to define the nature of that sympathy which exists between a well-bitted horse and his rider, they seem actuated by a common impulse, and it is to promote or create this mutual understanding that so many remarkable conceits, generally painful, have been

33

dignified with the name of bridles. In the saddle-room of any hunting man may be found at least a dozen of these, but you will probably learn on inquiry, that three or four at most are all he keeps in use. It must be a stud of strangely - varying mouths and tempers which the snaffle, gag, Pelham, and double-bridle are insufficient to humour and control.

As it seems from the oldest representations known of men on horseback, to have been the earliest in use, we will take the snaffle first.

This bit, the invention of common-sense going straight to its object, while lying easily on the tongue and bars of a horse's mouth, and affording control without pain, is perfection of its kind. It causes no annoyance and consequently no alarm to the unbroken colt, champing and churning freely at the new plaything between his jaws; on it the highly-trained charger bears pleasantly and lightly, to "change his leg,"—"passage,"—or "shoulder in," at the slightest inflection of a rider's hand; the hunter leans against it for support in deep ground; and the race-horse allows it to hold him together at nearly full speed without contracting his stride, or by fighting with the restriction wasting any of his gallop in the air. It answers its purpose admirably *so long as it remains in the proper place*, but not a moment longer. Directly a horse by sticking out his nose can shift this pressure to his lips and teeth, it affords no more control than a halter. With head up, and mouth open, he can go how and where he will. In such a predicament only an experienced horseman has the skill to give him such an amount of liberty without licence as cajoles him into dropping again to his bridle, before he breaks away. Once off at speed, with the conviction that he is master, however ludicrous in appearance, the affair is serious enough in fact.

Many centuries elapsed, and a good deal of unpleasant riding must have been endured, before the snaffle was supplemented with a martingale. Judging from the Elgin Marbles, this useful invention seems to have been wholly unknown to the Greeks. Though the men's figures are perfect in seat and attitude through the whole of that spirited frieze which adorned the Parthenon, not one of their horses carries its head in the right place. The ancient Greek seems to have relied on strength rather than cunning, in his dealings with the noble animal, and though he sat down on it like a workman, must have found considerable difficulty in guiding his beast the way he wanted to go.

But with a martingale, the most insubordinate soon discover that they cannot rid themselves of control. It keeps their heads down in a position that enables the bit to act on the mouth, and if they must needs pull, obliges them to pull against that most sensitive part called the bars. There is no escape—bend their necks they must, and to bend their necks means to acknowledge a master and do homage to the rider's will.

It is a well-known fact, and I can attest it by my own experience, that a *twisted* snaffle with a martingale will hold a runaway when every other bridle fails; but to guide or stop an animal by the exercise of bodily strength is not horsemanship, and to saw at its mouth for the purpose cannot be expected to promote that sympathy of desire and intention which we understand by the term.

If we look at the sporting prints of our grandfathers and great - grandfathers, as delineated, early in the present century, we observe that nine out of every ten hunters were ridden in plain snaffle bridles, and we ask ourselves if our progenitors bred more docile beasts, or were these drinkers of port wine, bolder, stronger, and better horsemen than their descendants. Without entering on the vexed question of comparative merit in hounds, hunters, pace, country, and sport, at an interval of more than two generations, I think I can find a reason, and it seems to me simply this.

Most of these hunting pictures are representations of the chase in our midland counties, notably

THE USE OF THE BRIDLE

Leicestershire and Northamptonshire, then only partially enclosed; boundary fences of large properties were few and far between, straggling also, and ill-made-up, the high thorn hedges that now call forth so much bold and so much timid riding, either did not exist, or were of such tender growth as required protection by a low rail on each side, and a sportsman, with flying coat-tails, doubling these obstacles neatly, at his own pace, forms a favourite subject for the artist of the time. Twenty or thirty horsemen, at most, comprised the field; in such an expanse of free country there must have been plenty of room to ride, and we all know how soon a horse becomes amenable to control on a moor or an open down. The surface, too, was undrained, and a few furlongs bring the hardest puller to reason when he goes in over his fetlocks every stride. Hand and heel are the two great auxiliaries of the equestrian, but our grandfathers, I imagine, made less use of the bridle than the spur.

With increased facilities for locomotion, in the improvement of roads and coaches, hunting, always the English gentleman's favourite pastime, became a passion for everyone who could afford to keep a horse, and men thought little of twelve hours spent in the mail on a dark winter's night in order to meet hounds next day. The numbers attending a favourite fixture began to multiply, second horses were introduced, so that long before the use of railways scarlet coats mustered by tens as to-day by fifties, and the *crowd*, as it is called, became a recognised impediment to the enjoyments of the day.

Meantime fences were growing in height and thickness; an improved system of farming subdivided the fields and partitioned them off for pastoral or agricultural purposes; the hunter was called upon to collect himself, and jump at short notice, with a frequency that roused his mettle to the utmost, and this, too, in a rush of his fellow-creatures, urging, jostling, crossing him in the first five minutes at every turn.

Under such conditions it became indispensable to have him in perfect control, and that excellent invention, the double-bridle, came into general use.

I suppose I need hardly explain to my reader that it loses none of the advantages belonging to the snaffle, while it gains in the powerful leverage of the curb a restraint few horses are resolute enough to defy. In skilful hands, varying, yet harmonising, the manipulation of both, as a musician plays treble and bass on the pianoforte, it would seem to connect the rider's thought with the horse's movement, as if an electric chain passed through wrist, and finger, and mouth, from the head of the one to the heart of the other.

THE USE OF THE BRIDLE

The bearing and touch of this instrument can be so varied as to admit of a continual change in the degree of liberty and control, of that give-and-take which is the whole secret of comfortable progression. While the bridoon or snaffle-rein is tightened, the horse may stretch his neck to the utmost, without losing that confidence in the moral support of his rider's hand which is so encouraging to him if unaccompanied by pain. When the curb is brought into play, he bends his neck at its pressure to a position that brings his hind legs under his own body and his rider's weight, from which collected form alone can his greatest efforts be made. Have your curb-bit sufficiently powerful, if not high in the *port*, at any rate long in the *cheek*, your bridoon as thick as your saddler can be induced to send it. With the first you bring a horse's head into the right place; with the second, if smooth and *very* thick, you keep it there, in perfect comfort to the animal, and consequently to yourself. A thin bridoon, and I have seen them mere wires, only cuts, chafes, and irritates, causing more pain and consequently more resistance, than the curb itself. I have already mentioned the fineness of Mr. Lovell's hand (alas! that he has but one), and I was induced by this gentleman to try a plan of his own invention, which, with his delicate manipulation, he found to be a success. Instead of the usual bridoon, he rode with a double strap of leather, exactly the width of a bridle-rein, and twice its thickness, resting where the snaffle ordinarily lies, on the horse's tongue and bars. With his touch it answered admirably; with mine, perhaps because I used the leather more roughly than the metal, it seemed the severer of the two. But a badly-broken horse, and half the hunters we ride have scarcely been taught their alphabet, will perhaps try to avoid the restraint of a curb by throwing his head up at the critical moment when you want to steady him for a difficulty. If you have a firm seat, perfectly independent of the bridle,—and do not be too sure of this, until you have tried the experiment of sitting a leap with nothing to hold on by,—you may call in the assistance of the running martingale, slipping your curb-rein, which should be made to unbuckle, through its rings. Your *curb*, I repeat, contrary to the usual practice, and *not your snaffle*. I will soon explain why.

The horse has so docile a nature, that he would always rather do right than wrong, if he can only be taught to distinguish one from the other; therefore, have all your restrictive power on the same engine. Directly he gives to your hand, by affording him more liberty you show him that he has met your wishes, and done what you asked. If you put the martingale on your bridoon rein, you can no longer indicate approval. To avoid its control he must lean on the discomfort of his curb, and it puzzles no less than it discourages him, to find that every effort to please you is met, one way or the other, by restraint. So much for his convenience ; now for your own. I will suppose you are using the common hunting martingale, attached to the breastplate of your saddle, not to its girths. Be careful that the rings are too small to slip over those of the curbbit ; you will be in an awkward predicament if, after rising at a fence, your horse in the moment that he tries to extend himself finds his nose tied down to his knees.

Neither must you shorten it too much at first : rather accustom your pupil gradually to its restraint, and remember that all horses are not shaped alike ; some are so formed that they must needs carry their heads higher, and, as you choose to think, in a worse place than others. Tuition in all its branches cannot be too gradual, and nature, whether of man or beast, is less easily driven than led. The first consideration in riding is, no doubt, to make our horses do what we desire ; but when this elementary object has been gained, it is of great importance to our comfort that they should accept our wishes as their own, persuaded that they exert themselves voluntarily in the service of their riders. For this it is essential to use such a bridle as they do not fear to meet, yet feel unwilling to disobey. Many high-couraged horses, with sensitive mouths, no uncommon combination, and often united to those propelling powers in hocks and quarters that are so valuable to a hunter, while they scorn restraint by the mild influence of the snaffle, fight tumultuously against the galling restriction of a curb. For these the scion of a noble family, that has produced many fine riders, invented a bridle, combining, as its enemies declare, the defects of both, to which he has given his name.

In England there seems a very general prejudice against the Pelham, whereas in Ireland we see it in constant use. Like other bridles of a peculiar nature, it is adapted for peculiar horses; and I have myself had three or four excellent hunters that would not be persuaded to go comfortably in anything else.

I need hardly explain the construction of a Pelham. It consists of a single bit, smooth and jointed, like a common snaffle, but prolonged from the rings on either side to a cheek, having a second rein attached, which acts, by means of a curb-chain round the lower jaw, in the same manner, though to a modified extent, as the curb-rein of the usual hunting double-bridle, to which it bears an outward resemblance, and of which it

THE USE OF THE BRIDLE

seems a mild and feeble imitation. I have never
to this day made out whether or not a keen young
sportsman was amusing himself at my expense,
when, looking at my horse's head thus equipped,
he asked the simple question: "Do you find it
a good plan to have your snaffle and curb all in
one?" I *did* find it a good plan with that
particular horse, and at the risk of appearing
egotistical I will explain why, by narrating the
circumstances under which I first discovered
his merits, illustrating as they do the special
advantages of this unpopular implement.

The animal in question, thoroughbred, and
amongst hunters exceedingly speedy, was unused
to jumping when I purchased him, and from his
unaffected delight in their society, I imagine had
never seen hounds. He was active, however,
high-couraged, and only too willing to be in front;
but with a nervous, excitable temperament, and
every inclination to pull hard, he had also a
highly sensitive mouth. The double-bridle in
which he began his experiences annoyed him sadly;
he bounced, fretted, made himself thoroughly
disagreeable, and our first day was a pleasure to
neither of us. Next time I bethought me of
putting on a Pelham, and the effect of its greater
liberty seemed so satisfactory, that to enhance it
I took the curb-chain off altogether. I was in
the act of pocketing the links, when a straight-

necked fox broke covert, pointing for a beautiful
grass country, and the hounds came pouring out
with a burning scent, not five hundred yards from
his brush. I remounted pretty quick, but my
thoroughbred one—in racing language "a good
beginner"—was quicker yet, and my feet were
hardly in the stirrups, ere he had settled to his
stride, and was flying along in rather too close
proximity to the pack. Happily, there was
plenty of room, and the hounds ran unusually
hard, for my horse fairly broke away with me in
the first field, and although he allowed me by
main force to steady him a little at his fences,
during ten minutes at least I know who was *not*
master! He calmed, however, before the end of
the burst, which was a very brilliant gallop, over
a practicable country, and when I sent him home
at two o'clock, I felt satisfied I had a game, good
horse, that would soon make a capital hunter.

Now I am persuaded our timely *escapade* was
of the utmost service. It gave him confidence in
his rider's hand; which with this light Pelham
bridle he found could inflict on him no pain, and
only directed him the way he delighted to go.
On his next appearance in the hunting-field, he
was not afraid to submit to a little more restraint,
and so by degrees, though I am bound to admit
the process took more than one season, he became
a steady, temperate conveyance, answering the

powerful conventional double-bridle with no less docility than the most sedate of his stable companions. We have seen a great deal of fun together since, but never such a game of romps as our first!

Why are so many brilliant horses difficult to ride? It ought not to be so. The truest shape entails the truest balance, consequently the smoothest paces and the best mouth. The fault is neither of form nor temper, but originates, if truth must be told, in the prejudices of the breaker, who will not vary his system to meet the requirements of different pupils. The best hunters have necessarily great power behind the saddle, causing them to move with their hind legs so well under them, that they will not, and indeed cannot lean on the rider's hand. This the breaker calls "facing their bit," and the shyer they seem of that instrument, the harder he pulls. Up go their heads to avoid the pain, till that effort of self-defence becomes a habit, and it takes weeks of patience and fine horsemanship to undo the effects of unnecessary ill-usage for an hour.

Eastern horses, being broke from the first in the severest possible bits, all acquire this trick of throwing their noses in the air; but as they have never learned to pull, for the Oriental prides himself on riding with a finger, you need only give them an easy bridle and a martingale to make them go quietly and pleasantly, with heads in the right place, delighted to find control not necessarily accompanied by pain.

And this indeed is the whole object of our numerous inventions. A light-mouthed horse steered by a good rider, will cross a country safely and satisfactorily in a Pelham bridle, with a running martingale on the *lower* rein. It is only necessary to give him his head at his fences, that is to say, to let his mouth alone, the moment he leaves the ground. That the man he carries can hold a horse up, while landing, I believe to be a fallacy; that he gives him every chance in a difficulty by sitting well back and not interfering with his efforts to recover himself, I know to be a fact. The rider cannot keep too quiet till the last moment, when his own knee touches the ground, then the sooner he parts company the better, turning his face towards his horse if possible, so as not to lose sight of the falling mass, and, above all, holding the bridle in his hand.

The last precaution cannot be insisted on too strongly. Not to mention the solecism of being afoot in boots and breeches during a run, and the cruel tax we inflict on some brother-sportsman, who, being too good a fellow to leave us in the lurch, rides his own horse furlongs out of his line to go and catch ours, there is the further consideration of personal safety to life and limb. That is a very false position in which a man finds himself, when the animal is on its legs again, who cannot clear his foot from the stirrup, and has let his horse's head go!

I believe, too, that a tenacious grasp on the reins saves many a broken collar-bone, as it cants the rider's body round in the act of falling, so that the cushion of muscle behind it, rather than the point of his shoulder, is the first place to touch the ground, and no one who has ever been "pitched into" by a bigger boy at school can have forgotten that this part of the body takes punishment with the greatest impunity. But we are wandering from our subject. To hold on like grim death when down, seems an accomplishment little akin to the contents of a chapter professing to deal with the skilful use of the bridle.

The horse, except in peculiar cases, such as a stab with a sharp instrument, shrinks like other animals from pain. If he cannot avoid it in one way he will in another. When suffering under the pressure of his bit, he endeavours to escape the annoyance, according to the shape and setting on of his neck and shoulders, either by throwing his head up to the level of a rider's eyes, or dashing it down between his own knees. The latter is by far the most pernicious manœuvre of the two, and to counteract it has been constructed the instrument we call "a gag."

This is neither more nor less than another snaffle bit, of which the head-stall and rein, instead of being separately attached to the rings, are in one piece running through a swivel, so that a leverage is obtained on the side of the mouth of such power as forces the horse's head upwards to its proper level. In a gag and snaffle no horse can continue "boring," as it is termed, against his rider's hand; in a gag and curb he is indeed a hard puller who will attempt to run away.

But with this bridle, adieu to all those delicacies of fingering which form the great charm of horsemanship, and are indeed the master-touches of the art. A gag cannot be drawn gently through the mouth with hands parted and lowered on each side so as to "turn and wind a fiery Pegasus," nor is the bull-headed beast that requires it one on which, without long and patient tuition, you may hope to "witch the world with noble horsemanship." It is at best but a school-master, and like the curbless Pelham in which my horse ran away with me, only a step in the right direction towards such willing obedience as we require. Something has been gained when our horse learns we have power to control him; much when he finds that power exerted for his own advantage. I would ride mine in a chain-cable if by no other means I could make him understand that he must submit to my will, hoping always eventually to substitute for it a silken thread.

All bridles, by whatever names they may be called, are but the contrivances of a government that depends for authority on concealment of its weakness. Hard hands will inevitably make hard pullers, but to the animal intellect a force still untested is a force not lightly to be defied. The loose rein argues confidence, and even the brute understands that confidence is an attribute of power.

Change your bridle over and over again, till you find one that suits your hand, rather, I should say, that suits your horse's mouth. Do not, however, be too well satisfied with a first essay. He may go delightfully to-day in a bit that he will learn how to counteract by to-morrow. Nevertheless, a long step has been made in the right direction when he has carried you pleasantly if only for an hour. Should that period have been passed in following hounds, it is worth a whole week's education under less exciting conditions. A horse becomes best acquainted with his rider in those situations that call forth most care and circumspection from both.

Broken ground, fords, morasses, dark nights, all tend to mutual good understanding, but forty minutes over an enclosed country establishes the partnership of man and beast on such relations of confidence as much subsequent indiscretion fails to efface. The same excitement that rouses his courage seems to sharpen his faculties and clear his brain. It is wonderful how soon he begins to understand your meaning as conveyed literally from "hand to mouth," how cautiously he picks his steps amongst stubs or rabbit-holes, when the loosened rein warns him he must look out for himself, how boldly he quickens his stride and collects his energies for the fence he is approaching, when he feels grip and grasp tighten on back and bridle, conscious that you mean to "catch hold of his head and send him at it!" while loving you all the better for this energy of yours that stimulates his own.

And now we come to a question admitting of no little discussion, inasmuch as those practitioners differ widely who are best capable of forming an opinion. The advocates of the loose rein, who though outnumbered at the covert-side, are not always in a minority when the hounds run, maintain that a hunter never acquits himself so well as while let completely alone; their adversaries, on the other hand, protest that the first principle of equitation is, to keep fast hold of your horse's head at all times and under all circumstances.

THE USE OF THE BRIDLE

" You pull him into his fences," argues Finger.

" *You* will never pull him out of them," answers Fist.

"Get into a bucket and try to lift yourself by the handles!" rejoins Finger, quoting from an apposite illustration of Colonel Greenwood's, as accomplished a horseman as his brother, also a colonel, whose fine handling I have already mentioned.

"A horse isn't a bucket," returns Fist triumphantly; "why, directly you let his head go, does he stop in a race, refuse a brook, or stumble when tired on the road?"

It is a thousand pities that he cannot tell us which of the two systems he prefers himself. We may argue from theory, but can only judge by practice, and must draw our inferences rather from personal experience than the subtlest reasoning of the schools.

Now if all horses were broke by such masters of the art as General Lawrenson and Mr. Mackenzie Greaves, riders who combine the strength and freedom of the hunting - field with the scientific exercise of hands and limbs, as taught in the *haute école*, so obedient would they become to our gestures, nay, to the inflection of our bodies, that they might be trusted over the strongest lordship in Leicestershire with their heads quite loose, or, for that matter, with no bridle at all. But equine education is usually conducted on a very different system to that of Monsieur Baucher, or either of the above-named gentlemen. From colthood horses have been taught to understand, paradoxically enough, that a dead pull against the jaws means, "Go on, and be hanged to you, till I alter the pressure as a hint for you to stop."

It certainly seems common-sense, that when we tug at a horse's bridle he should oblige us by coming to a halt, yet, in his fast paces, we find the pull produces a precisely contrary effect; and for this habit, which during the process of breaking has become a second nature, we must make strong allowances, particularly in the hurry and excitement of crossing a country after a pack of hounds.

It has happened to most of us, no doubt, at some period to have owned a favourite, whose mouth was so fine, temper so perfect, courage so reliable, and who had so learned to accommodate pace and action to our lightest indications, that when thus mounted we felt we could go tit-tupping over a country with slackened rein and toe in stirrup, as if cantering in the Park. As we near our fence, a little more forbidding, perhaps, than common, every stride seems timed like clockwork, and, unwilling to interfere with such perfect mechanism, we drop our hand, trusting wholly

in the honour of our horse. At the very last
stride the traitor refuses, and whisks round.
"*Et tu brute!*" we exclaim—"Are *you* also a
brute?"—and catching him vigorously by the
head, we ram him again at the obstacle to fly
over it like a bird. Early associations had
prevailed, and our stanch friend disappointed us,
not from cowardice, temper, nor incapacity, but
only from the influence of an education based on
principles contrary to common-sense.

The great art of horsemanship, then, is to find
out what the animal requires of us, and to meet
its wishes, even its prejudices, half-way. Cool
with the rash, and daring with the cautious, it is
wise to retain the semblance, at least, of a self-
possession superior to casualties, and equal to
any emergency, from a refusal to a fall. Though
"give and take" is the very first principle of
handling, too sudden a variation of pressure has
a tendency to confuse and flurry a hunter,
whether in the gallop or when collecting itself
for the leap. If you have been holding a horse
hard by the head, to let him go in the last stride
is very apt to make him run into his fence; while,
if you have been riding with a light hand and
loosened rein, a "chuck under the chin" at an
inopportune moment distracts his attention, and
causes him to drop short. "How did you get
your fall?" is a common question in the hunting-

field. If the partner at one end of the bridle could speak, how often would he answer, " Through bad riding ;" when the partner at the other dishonestly replies, " The brute didn't jump high enough, or far enough, that was all." It is well for the most brilliant reputations that the noble animal is generous as he is brave, and silent as he is wise.

I have already observed there are many more kinds of bridles than those just mentioned. Major Dwyer's, notably, of which the principle is an exact fitting of bridoon and curb-bits to the horse's mouth, seems to give general satisfaction ; and Lord Gardner, whose opinion none are likely to dispute, stamps it with his approval. I confess, however, to a preference for the old-fashioned double-bridles, such as are called respectively the Dunchurch, Nos. 1 and 2, being persuaded that these will meet the requirements of nine horses out of ten that have any business in the hunting-field. The first, very large, powerful, and of stronger leverage than the second, should be used with discretion, but, in good hands, is an instrument against which the most resolute puller, if he insists on fighting with it, must contend in vain. Thus tackled, and ridden by such a horseman as Mr. Angerstein, for instance, of Weeting, in Norfolk, I do not believe there are half a dozen hunters in England that could get the mastery. Whilst living in Northampton-shire I remember he owned a determined runaway, not inappropriately called "Hard Bargain," that in this bridle he could turn and twist like a pony. I have no doubt he has not forgotten the horse, nor a capital run from Misterton, in which, with his usual kindness, he lent him thus bridled to a friend.

I have seen horses go very pleasantly in what I believe is called the half-moon bit, of which the bridoon, having no joint, is shaped so as to take the curve of the animal's mouth. I have never tried one, but the idea seems good, as based on the principle of comfort to the horse. When we can arrive at that essential, combined with power to the rider, we may congratulate ourselves on possessing the right bridle at last, and need have no scruple in putting the animal to its best pace, confident we can stop it at will.

We should never forget that the faster hounds run, the more desirable is it to have perfect control of our conveyance; and that a hunter of very moderate speed, easy to turn, and quick on its legs, will cross a country with more expedition than a race-horse that requires half a field to "go about"; and that we dare not extend lest, "with too much way on," he should get completely out of our hand. Once past the gap you fancied, you will never find a place in the fence you like so well again.

CHAPTER IV

THE ABUSE OF THE SPUR

"You may ride us,
With one soft kiss, a thousand furlongs, ere
With spurs we heat an acre"—

SAYS Hermione, and indeed that gentle lady's illustration equally applies to an inferior order of beings, from which also man derives much comfort and delight. It will admit of discussion whether the "armed heel," with all its terrors, has not, on the racecourse at least, lost more triumphs than it has won.

I have been told that Fordham, who seems to be first past the judges' chair oftener than any jockey of the day, wholly repudiates "the tormentors," arguing that they only make a horse shorten his stride, and "shut up," to use an expressive term, instead of struggling gallantly home. Judging by analogy, it is easy to conceive that such may be the case. The tendency of the human frame seems certainly to contract rather than expand its muscles, with instinctive repugnance at the stab of a sharp instrument, or even the puncture of a thorn. It is not while receiving punishment but administering it that the prize-fighter opens his shoulders and lets out. There is no doubt that many horses, thoroughbred ones especially, will stop suddenly, even in their gallop, and resent by kicking an indiscreet application of the spurs. A determined rider who keeps them screwed in the animal's flanks eventually gains the victory. But such triumphs of severity and main force are the last resource of an authority that ought never to be disputed, as springing less from fear than confidence and goodwill.

It cannot be denied that there are many fools in the world, yet, regarding matters of opinion, the majority are generally right. A top-boot has an unfinished look without its appendage of shining steel; and, although some sportsmen assure us they dispense with rowels, it is rare to find one so indifferent to appearances as not to wear spurs. There must be some good reason for this general adoption of an instrument that, from the days of chivalry, has been the very stamp and badge of a superiority which the man on horseback assumes over the man on foot. Let us weigh the arguments for and against this emblem of knighthood before we decide. In the riding-school, and particularly for military purposes, when the dragoon's right hand is required for his weapon, these aids, as they are called, seem to enhance that pressure of the leg which acts on the horse's quarters, as the rein on his forehand, bringing his whole body into the required position. Perhaps if the boot were totally unarmed much time might be lost in making his pupil understand the horseman's wishes, but anyone who has ridden a perfectly trained charger knows how much more accurately it answers to the leg than the heel, and how awkwardly a horse acquits himself that has been broke in very sharp spurs; every touch causing it to wince and swerve too far in the required direction, glancing off at a tangent, like a boat that is over ready in answering her helm. Patience and a light switch, I believe, would fulfil all the purposes of the spur, even in the *manège*; but delay is doubtless a drawback, and there are reasons for going the shortest way on occasion, even if it be not the smoothest and the best.

It is quite unnecessary, however, and even prejudicial, to have the rowels long and sharp. Nothing impedes tuition like fear; and fear in the animal creation is the offspring of pain.

Granted, then, that the spur may be applied advantageously in the school, let us see how far it is useful on the road or in the hunting-field.

We will start by supposing that you do not

possess a really perfect hack; that desirable animal must, doubtless, exist somewhere, but, like Pegasus, is more often talked of than seen. Nevertheless, the roadster that carries you to business or pleasure is a sound, active, useful beast, with safe, quick action, good shoulders, of course, and a willing disposition, particularly when turned towards home. How often in a week do you touch it with the spurs? Once, perhaps, by some bridle-gate, craftily hung at precisely the angle which prevents your reaching its latch or hasp. And what is the result of this little display of vexation? Your hack gets flurried, sticks his nose in the air, refuses to back, and compels you at last to open the gate with your wrong hand, rubbing your knee against the post as he pushes through in unseemly haste, for fear of another prod. When late for dinner, or hurrying home to outstrip the coming shower, you may fondly imagine that but for "the persuaders" you would have been drenched to the skin; and, relating your adventures at the fireside, will probably declare that "you stuck the spurs into him the last mile, and came along as hard as he could drive." But, if you were to visit him in the stable, you would probably find his flanks untouched, and would, I am sure, be pleased rather than disappointed at the discovery. Happily, not one man in ten knows *how* to spur

a horse, and the tenth is often the most unwilling
to administer so severe a punishment.

Ladies, however, are not so merciful.   Perhaps
because they have but one, they use this stimulant
liberally, and without compunction.   From their
seat, and shortness of stirrup, every kick tells
home.   Concealed under a riding-habit, these
vigorous applications are unsuspected by lookers-
on ; and the unwary wonder why, in the streets
of London or the Park, a ladies' horse always
appears to go in a lighter and livelier form than
that of her male companion.   " It's a woman's
hand," says the admiring pedestrian.   " Not a
bit of it," answers the cynic who knows ; " it's a
woman's heel."

But, however sparing you may be of the spurs
in lane or bridle-road, you are tempted to ply
them far too freely in the anxiety and excitement
of the hunting-field.   Have you ever noticed the
appearance of a white horse at the conclusion of
some merry gallop over a strongly fenced country ?
The pure conspicuous colour tells sad tales, and
the smooth, thin-skinned flanks are too often
stained and plastered with red.   Many bad horsemen spur their horses without meaning it ; many
worse, mean to spur their horses at every fence,
and *do*.

A Leicestershire notability, of the last generation, once dubbed a rival with the expressive title

of "a hard funker"; and the term, so happily
applied, fully rendered what he meant. Of all
riders the hard funker is the most unmerciful to
his beast; at every turn he uses his spurs cruelly,
not because he is *hard*, but because he *funks*.
Let us watch him crossing a country, observing
his style as a warning rather than an example.

Hesitation and hurry are his principal faults,
practised, with much impartiality, in alternate
extremes. Though half-way across a field, he is
still undecided where to get out. This vacillation
communicates itself in electric sympathy to his
horse, and both go wavering down to their fence,
without the slightest idea what they mean to do
when they arrive. Some ten strides off the
rider makes up his mind, selecting, probably, an
extremely awkward place, for no courage is so
desperate as that which is founded on fear.
Want of determination is now supplemented by
excessive haste, and with incessant application of
the spurs his poor horse is hurried wildly at the
leap. That it gets over without falling, as
happens oftener than might be supposed, seems
due to activity in the animal rather than sagacity
in the rider, and a strong instinct of self-preservation in both; but such a process, repeated again
and again during a gallop, even of twenty
minutes, tells fearfully on wind and muscle, nor
have many hunters sufficient powers of endurance

to carry these exacting performers through a run.

Still the "h. f." would be nothing without his spurs, and I grant that to him these instruments are indispensable, if he is to get from one field to another; but of what use are they to such men as Mr. Gilmour, Captain Coventry, Sir Frederic Johnston, Captain Boyce, Mr. Hugh Lowther, and a host more that I could name, who seem to glide over Leicestershire, and other strongly-fenced countries, as a bird glides through the air? Day after day, unless accidentally scored in a fall, you may look in vain for a spur-mark on their horses' sides. Shoulders and quarters, indeed, are reddened by gashes from a hundred thorns; but the virgin spot, a handsbreadth behind the girths, is pure and stainless still. Yet not one of the gentlemen I have named will ride without the instrument he uses so rarely, if at all; and they must cherish, therefore, some belief in its virtue, when called into play, strong enough to counterbalance its indisputable disadvantages—notably, the stabbing of a hunter's side, when its rider's foot is turned outwards by a stake or grower, and the tearing of its back or quarters in the struggle and confusion of a fall. There is one excellent reason that, perhaps, I may have overlooked. It is tiresome to answer the same question over and over again, and in a field of two hundred sportsmen you are sure to be asked almost as many times, "Why don't you wear spurs?" if you set appearances at defiance by coming into the hunting-field without them.

In my personal recollection I can only call to mind one man who systematically abjured so essential a finish to the horseman's dress and equipment. This was Mr. Tomline of Leigh Lodge, a Leicestershire farmer and horse-dealer, well known some thirty years ago as one of the finest riders and straightest goers that ever got into a saddle. His costume, indeed, was not of so careful a nature that want of completeness in any one particular could spoil the general effect. He *always* hunted in a rusty, worn pilot-jacket, drab breeches with strings untied, brown-topped boots, and a large ill-fitting hat, carrying in his hand a ground-ash plant, totally useless for opening a gate if he did not happen to jump it. Yet thus accoutred, and generally on a young one, so long as his horse's condition lasted, he was sure to be in front, and, when the fences were rougher than common, with but two or three companions at most.

I have not yet forgotten the style in which I once saw him coax a four-year-old to jump a "bottom" under Launde, fortified by a high post and rail—downhill—a bad take-off—and almost a ravine on the far side! With his powerful grip and exquisite handling, he seemed to persuade the pupil that it was as willing as the master.

My own spurs were four inches long, and I was riding the best hunter in my stable, but I don't think I would have had the same place for fifty pounds!

A paradox, like an Irishman's bull, will sometimes convey our meaning more impressively than a logical statement. It seems paradoxical, yet I believe it is sound sense, to say that no man should arm his heels with spurs unless he is so good a rider as to be sure they shall not touch his horse. To punish him with them involuntarily is, of course, like any other blunder totally inadmissible, but when applied with intention, they should be used sparingly and only as a last resource. That there *are* occasions on which they rouse a horse's energies for a momentary effort, I am disposed to admit, less from my own experience than the opinion of those for whose practical knowledge in all such matters I have the greatest respect. Both the Messrs. Coventry, in common with other first-rate steeplechase riders, advocate their use on rare occasions and under peculiar circumstances. Poor Jem Mason never went hunting without them, and would not, I think, have hesitated to apply them pretty freely if required, but then these could all spur their horses in the right place, leaning back the while and altering in no way the force and bearing of hand or seat. Most men, on the contrary, stoop forward and let their horses' heads go when engaged in this method of compulsion, and even if their heels *do* reach the mark, by no means a certainty, gain but little with the rowels compared to all they lose with the reins.

There is no fault in a hunter so annoying to a man whose heart is in the sport as a tendency to refuse. It utterly defeats the timid and damps the courage of the bold, while even to him who rides that he may hunt rather than hunts that he may ride, it is intensely provoking, as he is apt to lose by it that start which is so invaluable in a quick thing, and, when a large field are all struggling for the same object, so difficult to regain. This perversity of disposition, too, is very apt to be displayed at some fence that will not admit of half-measures, such as a rail low enough to jump, but too strong to break, or a ditch so wide and deep that it must not be attempted as a standing leap. In these cases a vigorous dig with the spurs at the last moment will sometimes have an excellent effect. But it must not be trusted as an unfailing remedy. Nearly as many hunters will resent so broad a hint, by stopping short, and turning restive, as will spring generously forward, and make a sudden effort in answer to the appeal. For this, as for every other requirement of equitation, much depends on an insight into his character, whom an enthusiastic friend of mine designates "the bolder and wiser animal of the two."

Few men go out hunting with the expectation of encountering more than one or two falls in the best of runs, although the score sometimes increases very rapidly, when a good and gallant horse is getting tired towards the finish. Twenty croppers in a season, if he is well mounted, seems a high average for the most determined of bruisers ; but a man, whom circumstances impel to ride whatever he can lay hands on, must take into consideration how he can best rise from the ground unhurt with no less forethought than he asks his way to the meet or inquires into the condition of his mount. To such a bold rider the spur may seem an indispensable article, but he must remember that even if its application should save him on occasion, which I am not altogether prepared to admit, the appendage itself is most inconvenient when down. I cannot remember a single instance of a man's foot remaining fixed in the stirrup who was riding without spurs. I do not mean to say such a catastrophe is impossible, but I have good reason to know that the buckle on the instep, which when brightly polished imparts such a finish to the lustrous wrinkles of a well-made boot, is extremely apt to catch in the angle of the stirrup iron, and hold us fast at the very moment when it is most important to our safety we should be free.

I have headed this chapter " The Abuse of the Spur," because I hold that implement of horsemanship to be in general most unmercifully abused, so much so that I believe it would be far better for the majority of horses, and riders too, if it had never come into vogue. The perfect equestrian may be trusted indeed with rowels sharp and long as those that jingle at the Mexican's heels on his boundless prairies, but, as in the days of chivalry, these ornaments should be won by prowess to be worn with honour; and I firmly believe that nine out of every ten men who come out hunting would be better and more safely carried if they left their spurs at home.

CHAPTER V

HAND

WHAT is it? Intellect, nerve, sympathy, confidence, skill? None of these can be said to constitute this quality; rather it is a combination of all, with something superinduced that can only be called a magnetic affinity between the aggressive spirit of man and the ductile nature of the beast.

> " He spurred the old horse, and *he held him tight*,
> And leaped him out over the wall,"

says Kingsley, in his stirring ballad of " The Knight's Last Leap at Alten-ahr " ; and Kingsley, an excellent rider himself, thus described exactly how the animal should have been put at its formidable fence. Most poets would have let their horse's head go—the loose rein is a favourite method of making play in literature—and a fatal refusal must have been the result. The German Knight, however, whose past life seems to have been no less disreputable than his end was tragic, had not

> " Lived by the saddle for years a score,"

to fail in his horsemanship at the finish, and so, when he came to jump his last fence, negotiated it with no less skill than daring—grim, quiet, resolute, strong of seat, and firm of hand. The latter quality seems, however, much the rarer of the two. For ten men who can stick to the saddle like Centaurs, you will hardly find one gifted with that nicety of touch which horses so willingly obey, and which, if not inborn, seems as difficult to acquire by practice as the draughtsman's eye for outline, or the musician's ear for sound. Attention, reflection, painstaking, and common-sense can, nevertheless, do much; and, if the brain will only take the trouble to think, the clumsiest fingers that ever mismanaged a bridle may be taught in time to humour it like a silken thread.

I have been told, though I never tried the experiment, that if you take bold chanticleer from his perch, and, placing his bill on a table, draw from it a line of chalk by candle-light, the poor dazed fowl makes no attempt to stir from this imaginary bondage, persuaded that it is secured by a cord it has not strength enough to break. We should never get on horseback without remembering this unaccountable illusion; our control by means of the bridle is, in reality, little more substantial than the chalk-line that seems to keep the bird in durance. It should be our first

consideration so to manage the rein we handle as
never to give our horse the opportunity of dis-
covering our weakness and his own strength.

How is this to be effected? By letting his
head go, and allowing him to carry us where he
will? Certainly not, or we should have no need
for the bridle at all. By pulling at him, then,
with main strength, and trying the muscular
power of our arms against that of his shoulders
and neck? Comparing these relative forces
again, we are constrained to answer, Certainly
not; the art of control is essentially founded on
compromise. In riding, as in diplomacy, we must
always be ready to give an inch that we may take
an ell. The first principle of horsemanship is to
make the animal believe we can rule its wildest
mood; the next, to prevent, at any sacrifice, the
submission of this plausible theory to proof. You
get on a horse you have never seen before,
improperly bitted, we may fairly suppose, for
few men would think of wasting as many seconds
on their bridle as they devote minutes to their
boots and breeches. You infer, from his wild eye
and restless ear, that he is "a bit of a romp"; and
you observe, with some concern, that surrounding
circumstances, a race, a review, a coursing-
meeting, or a sure find, it matters little which,
are likely to rouse all the tumultuous propensities
of his nature. Obviously it would be exceedingly

bad policy to have the slightest misunderstanding. The stone of Sisyphus gathered impetus less rapidly than does a horse who is getting the better of his rider ; and John Gilpin was not the first equestrian, by a good many, for whom

> " The trot became a gallop soon,
> In spite of curb and rein."

" I am the owner, I wish I could say the *master*, of the four best hunters I ever had in my life," wrote one of the finest horsemen in Europe to a brother-proficient in the art ; and although so frank an avowal would have seemed less surprising from an inferior performer, his friend, who was also in the habit of riding anything, anywhere, and over everything, doubtless understood perfectly what he meant.

Now in equitation there can be no divided empire ; and the horse will most assuredly be master if the man is not. In the interests of good government, then, beware how you let your authority literally slip through your fingers, for, once lost, it will not easily be regained.

Draw your reins gently to an equal length, and ascertain the precise bearing on your horse's mouth that seems, while he is yet in a walk, to influence his action without offending his sensitiveness. But this cannot be accomplished with the hands alone ; these members, though supposed to be the prime agents of control, will

71

do little without the assistance of legs and knees pressing the sides and flanks of the animal, so as to urge him against the touch of his bit, from which he will probably show a tendency to recoil, and, as it is roughly called, "forcing him into his bridle."

The absence of this leg-power is an incalculable disadvantage to ladies, and affords the strongest reason, amongst many, why they should be mounted only on temperate and perfectly broken horses. How much oftener would they come to grief but that their seat compels them to ride with such long reins as insure light hands, and that their finer sympathy seems fully understood and gratefully appreciated by the most sympathetic of all the brute creation!

The style adopted by good horsewomen, especially in crossing a country, has in it much to be admired, something, also, to be deprecated and deplored. They allow their horses plenty of liberty, and certainly interfere but little with their heads, even at the greatest emergencies; but their ideas of pace are unreasonably liberal, and they are too apt to "chance it" at the fences, encouraging with voice and whip the haste that in the last few strides it is judicious to repress. It seems to me they are safer in a bank-and-ditch country than amongst the high strong fences of the grazing districts, where a horse must be roused

HAND

and held together that he may jump well up in the air, and extend himself afterwards, so as to cover the wide uncertainties he may find on the landing side. For a bank he is pretty sure to collect himself without troubling his rider ; and this is, perhaps, why Irishmen, as a general rule, use such light bridles.

Now, a woman cannot possibly bring her horse up to a high staked-and-bound fence, out of deep ground, with the strength and resolution of a man, whose very grip in the saddle seems to extort from the animal its utmost energies. Half-measures are fatal in a difficulty, and, as she seems unable to interfere with good effect, she is wise to let it alone.

We may learn from her, however, one of the most effective secrets of the whole art, and that is, to ride with long reins. "Always give them plenty of rope," said poor Jem Mason, when instructing a beginner ; and he certainly practised what he preached. I have seen his hands carried so high as to be level with his elbows, but his horse's head was always in the right place ; and to this must be attributed the fact that, while he rode to hounds straighter than anybody else, he got comparatively few falls. A man with long reins not only affords his horse greater liberty at his fences, but allows him every chance of recovery should he get into difficulties on landing, the rider

73

not being pulled with a jerk on the animal's neck and shoulders, so as to throw both of them down, when they ought to have got off with a scramble.

Let us return to the horse you have lately mounted, not without certain misgivings that he may be tempted to insubordination under the excitement of tumult, rivalry, or noise. When you have discovered the amount of repression, probably very slight, that he accepts without resentment, at a walk, increase your pace gradually, still with your legs keeping him well into his bridle, carrying your hands low down on his withers, and, if you take my advice, with a rein in each. You will find this method affords you great control of your horse's head, and enables you, by drawing the bit through his mouth, to counteract any arrangement on his part for a dead pull, which could have but one result. Should you, moreover, find it necessary to jump, you can thus hold him perfectly straight at his fences, so that he must either decline altogether or go exactly *where you put him*. Young, head-strong horses are exceedingly apt to swerve from the place selected for them, and to rise sideways at some strong bit of timber, or impracticable part of a bullfinch; and this is a most dangerous experiment, causing the worst kind of falls to which the sportsman is liable.

Riding thus two-handed, you will probably find

your new acquaintance "bends" to you in his canter better than in his trot, and if so, you may safely push him to a gallop, taking great care, however, not to let him extend himself too much. When he goes on his shoulders, he becomes a free agent; so long as his haunches are under him, you can keep him, as it is called, "in your hand."

There is considerable scope for thought in this exercise of manual skill, and it is always wise to save labour of body by use of brain. Take care, then, to have your front clear, so that your horse may flatter himself he is leading his comrades, when he will not give you half so much trouble to retain him in reasonable bounds. Strategy is here required no less than tactics, and horseman-ship even as regards the bridle is quite as much a matter of head as hand. If you are out hunting, and have got thus far on good terms, you will probably now be tempted to indulge in a leap. We cannot, unfortunately, select these obstacles exactly as we wish; it is quite possible your first fence may be high, strong, and awkward, with every probability of a fall. Take your horse at it quietly, but resolutely, in a canter, remembering that the quicker and *shorter* his strides, while gathering *impetus*, the greater effort he can make when he makes his spring. Above all, measure with your eye, and endeavour to show him by the clip of your thighs, and the sway of your body, exactly where he should take off. On this important point depends, almost entirely, the success of your leap. Half a stride means some six or seven feet; to leave the ground that much too soon adds the width of a fair-sized ditch to his task, and if the sum total prove too much for him you cannot be surprised at the result. This is, I think, one of the most important points in horsemanship as applied to riding across a country. It is a detail in which Lord Wilton particularly excels, and although so good a huntsman must despise a compliment to his mere riding, I cannot refrain from mentioning Tom Firr, as another proficient who possesses this enviable knack in an extraordinary degree.

Many of us can remember "Cap" Tomline, a professional "rough rider," living at or near Billesdon, within the last twenty years, as fine a horseman as his namesake, whom I have already mentioned, and a somewhat lighter weight. For one sovereign, "Cap," as we used to call him, was delighted to ride anybody's horse under any circumstances, over, or into any kind of fence the owner chose to point out. After going brilliantly through a run, I have seen him, to my mind most injudiciously, desired to lark home alongside, while we watched his performance from the road. He was particularly fond of timber, and notwithstanding that his horse was usually rash, inexperienced, or bad - tempered, otherwise he would not have been riding him, I can call to mind very few occasions on which I saw him down.   One unusually open winter, when he hunted five and six days a week from October to April, he told me he had only fifteen falls, and that taking the seasons as they came, thirteen was about his average.   Nor was he a very light-weight—spare, lengthy, and muscular, he turned twelve stone in his hunting clothes, which were by no means of costly material.   Horses rarely refused with him, and though they often had a scramble for it, as seldom fell, but under his method of riding, sitting well down in the saddle, with the reins in both hands, they never took off wrong, and in this lay the great secret of his superiority.   When I knew him he was an exceedingly temperate man ; for many years I believe he drank only water, and he eschewed tobacco in every form.   "The reason you gentlemen have such *bad nerves*," he said to me, jogging home to Melton one evening in the dusk that always meets us about Somerby, "is because you smoke so much.   It turns your brains to a kind of vapour !"   The inference was startling, I thought, and not complimentary, but there might be some truth in it nevertheless.

We have put off a great deal of time at our

first fence, let us do it without a fall, if we can.

When a hunter's quarters are under him in taking off, he has them ready to help him over any unforeseen difficulty that may confront him on the other side. Should there be a bank from which he can get a purchase for a second effort, he will poise himself on it lightly as a bird, or perhaps, dropping his hind legs only, shoot himself well into the next field, with that delightful elasticity which, met by a corresponding action of his rider's loins, imparts to the horseman such sensations of confidence and dexterity as are felt by some buoyant swimmer, wafted home on the roll of an incoming wave. Strong hocks and thighs, a mutual predilection for the chase, a bold heart between the saddle-flaps, another under the waistcoat, and a pair of light hands, form a combination that few fences after Christmas are strong enough or blind enough to put down.

And now please not to forget that soundest of maxims, applicable to all affairs alike by land or sea—"While she lies her course, let the ship steer herself." If your horse is going to his own satisfaction, do not be too particular that he should go entirely to yours. So long as you can steady him, never mind that he carries his head a little up or a little down. If he shakes it you know you have got him, and can pull him off in a hundred yards. Keep your hands quiet and not too low. It is a well-known fact, of which, however, many draughtsmen seem ignorant, that the horse in action never puts his fore feet beyond his nose. You need only watch the finish of a race to be satisfied of this, and indeed the Derby winner in his supreme effort is almost as straight as an old-fashioned frigate, from stem to stern, while a line dropped perpendicularly from his muzzle would exactly touch the tips of his toes. Now, if your hands are on each side of your horse's withers, you make him bend his neck so much as to contract his stride within three-quarter speed ; whereas, when you carry them about the level of your own hips, and nearly as far back, he has enough freedom of head to extend himself without getting beyond your control, and room besides to look about him, of which be sure he will avail himself for your mutual advantage.

I have ridden hunters that obviously found great pleasure in watching hounds, and, except to measure their fences, would never take their eyes off the pack from field to field, so long as we could keep it in sight. These animals, too, were invariably fine jumpers, free, generous, light-hearted, and as wise as they were bold.

I heard a very superior performer once remark, that he not only rode every horse differently, but he rode the same horse differently at every fence.

RIDING RECOLLECTIONS

All I can say is, he used to ride them all in the same place, well up with the hounds, but I think I understand what he meant. He had his system, of course, like every other master of the art, but it admitted of endless variations according to circumstances and the exigencies of the case. No man, I conclude, rides so fast at a wall as a brook, though he takes equal pains with his handling in both cases, if in a different way, nor would he deny a half-tired animal that support, amounting even to a dead pull, which might cause a hunter fresh out of his stable to imagine his utmost exertions were required forthwith. Nevertheless, whether "lobbing along" through deep ground at the punishing period, when we wish our fun was over, or fingering a rash one delicately for his first fence, a stile, we will say, downhill with a bad take-off, when we could almost wish it had not begun, we equally require such a combination of skill, science, and sagacity, or rather common-sense, as goes by the name of "hand." When the player possesses this quality in perfection, it is wonderful how much can be done with the instrument of which he holds the strings. I remember seeing the Reverend John Bower, an extraordinarily fine rider of the last generation, hand his horse over an ugly iron-bound stile, on to some stepping-stones, with a drop of six or seven feet, into a Leicestershire

80

"Watching his performances from the road"

lane, as calmly as if the animal had been a lady
whom he was taking out for a walk. He pulled
it back into a trot, sitting very close and quiet,
with his hand raised two or three inches above
the withers, and I can still recall, as if I had seen
it yesterday, the curve of neck and quarters, as,
gently mouthing the bit, that well-broken hunter
poised lightly for its spring, and landing in the
same collected form, picked its way daintily, step
by step, down the declivity, like a cat. There
was a large field out, but though Leicestershire
then, as now, had no lack of bold and jealous
riders, who could use heads, hands, and beyond
all, their heels, nobody followed him, and I think
the attempt was better left alone.

Another clergyman of our own day, whose
name I forbear mentioning, because I think he
would dislike it for professional reasons, has the
finest bridle-hand of anyone I know. " You good
man," I once heard a foreigner observe to this
gentleman, in allusion to his bold style of riding ;
" it no matter if you break your neck!" And
although I cannot look on the loss of such
valuable lives from the same point of view as this
Continental moralist, I may be permitted to
regret the present scarcity of clergymen in the
hunting-field. It redounds greatly to their credit,
for we know how many of them deny themselves
a harmless pleasure rather than offend the

" weaker brethren," but what a dog in the manger must the weaker brother be!

I have never heard that these "hunting parsons," as they are called, neglect the smallest detail of duty to indulge in their favourite sport, but when they *do* come out you may be sure to see them in the front rank. Can it be that the weaker brother is jealous of his pastor's superiority in the saddle? I hope not. At any rate it seems unfair to cavil at the enjoyment by another of the pursuit we affect ourselves. Let us show more even-handed justice, if not more charity, and endeavour at least to follow the good man's example in the parish, though we are afraid to ride his line across the fields.

It would be endless to enter on all the different styles of horsemanship in which fine hands are of the utmost utility. On the racecourse, for instance, it seems to an outsider that the whole performance of the jockey is merely a dead pull from end to end. But only watch the lightest urchin that is flung on a two-year-old to scramble home five furlongs as fast as ever he can come; you will soon be satisfied that even in these tumultuous flights there is room for the display of judgment, patience, though briefly tried, and manual skill. The same art is exercised on the light smooth snaffle, held in tenacious grasp, that causes the heavily-bitted charger to dance and "passage" in the school. It differs only in direction and degree. As much dexterity is required to prevent some playful flyer recently put in training from breaking out in a game of romps, when he ought to be minding his business in "the string," as to call forth the well-drilled efforts of a war-horse, answering wrist and leg with disciplined activity, ready to "rein back," "pass," "wheel,"—

> "And high curvet that not in vain,
> The sword-sway may descend amain
> On foeman's casque below."

Chifney, the great jockey of his day, wrote an elaborate treatise on handling, laying down the somewhat untenable position, that even a race-horse should be held as if with a silken thread.

I have noticed, too, that our best steeplechase riders have particularly fine hands when crossing a country with hounds; nor does their professional practice seem to make them over-hasty at their fences, when there is time to do these with deliberation. I imagine that to ride a steeple-chase well, over a strong line, is the highest possible test of what we may call "all-round" horsemanship. My own experience in the silk jacket has been of the slightest; and I confess that, like Falstaff with his reasons, I never fancied being rattled quite so fast at my fences "on compulsion."

83

RIDING RECOLLECTIONS

One of the finest pieces of riding I ever witnessed was in a steeplechase held at Melton, as long ago as the year 1864, when, happening to stand near the brook, *eighteen feet of water*, I observed my friend Captain Coventry come down at it. Choosing sound ground and a clear place, for it was already beginning to fill with numerous competitors, he set his horse going, at about a hundred yards from the brink, in the most masterly manner, increasing the pace resolutely but gradually, so as not to flurry or cause the animal to change his leg, nearly to full speed before he took off. I could not have believed it possible to make a horse go so fast in so collected a form; but with the rider's strength in the saddle, and perfectly skilful hands, he accomplished the feat, and got well over, I need hardly. say, in his stride.

But, although a fine "bridle-hand," as it is called, proves of such advantage to the horseman in the hurry-skurry of a steeplechase or a very quick thing with hounds, its niceties come more readily under the notice of an observer on the road than in the field. Perhaps the Ride in Hyde Park is the place of all others where this quality is most appreciated, and, shall we add? most rarely to be found. A perfect Park hack, that can walk or canter five miles an hour, no light criterion of action and balance, should also

"Handing his horse over"

HAND

be so well broke, and so well ridden, as to change
its leg, if asked to do so, at every stride. "With
woven paces," if not "with waving arms," I have
seen rider and horse threading in and out the
trees that bisect Rotten Row, without missing
one, for half a mile on end; the animal leading
with near or off leg, as it inclined to left or right,
guided only by the inflection of the rider's body,
and the touch, too light to be called a pressure,
of his knee and leg. How seldom does one see
a horse ridden properly round a corner! He is
usually allowed to turn on his shoulders, with his
hind legs too far back to be of the slightest
assistance if he slips or stumbles, and should the
foothold be greasy, as may happen in London
streets, down he comes flat on his side. Even at
a walk, or slow trot, he should be collected, and
his outer flank pressed inwards by his rider's heel,
so that the motive-power in hocks and thighs is
kept under his own body, and the weight on his
back. In the canter it stands to reason that he
should lead with the inner leg, otherwise it is
very possible he may cross the other over it, and
fall like a lump of lead.

I remember seeing the famous Lord Anglesey
ride his hack at that pace nineteen times out of
Piccadilly into Albemarle Street, before it turned
the corner exactly to his mind. The handsome
old warrior, who *looked* no less distinguished than

85

RIDING RECOLLECTIONS

he *was*, had, as we know, a cork leg, and its
oscillation no doubt interfered with those niceties
of horsemanship in which he delighted. Nevertheless at the twentieth trial he succeeded, and a
large crowd, collected to watch him, seemed glad
of an opportunity to give their Waterloo hero a
hearty cheer as he rode away.

Perhaps the finest pair of hands to be seen
amongst the frequenters of the Park in the
present day belong to Mr. Mackenzie Greaves,
a retired cavalry officer of our own service, who,
passionately fond of hunting and everything
connected with horses, has lately turned his
attention to the subtleties of the *haute école*,
nowhere better understood, by a select few, than
in Paris, where he usually resides. To watch
this gentleman on a horse he has broken in
himself, gliding through the crowd, as if by mere
volition, with the smoothness, ease, and rapidity
of a fish arrowing up a stream, makes one quite
understand how the myth of the Centaur
originated in the sculpture and poetry of
Greece.

In common with General Laurenson, whose
name I have already mentioned as just such
another proficient, his system is very similar to
that of Monsieur Baucher, one of the few lovers
of the animal either in France or England, who
have so studied its character as to reduce equine

86

education to a science. Its details are far too
elaborate to enter on here, but one of its first
principles, applied in the most elementary tuition,
is never to let the horse recoil from his bridle.

"Drop your hands!" say nine good riders out
of ten, when the pupil's head is thrown up to
avoid control. "Not so," replies Baucher. "On
the contrary, tighten and increase your pressure
more and more, keeping the rebel up to his bit
with legs and spurs if necessary, till *he* yields,
not you ; then on the instant, rapidly and dexter-
ously, as you would strike in fly-fishing, give to
him, and he will come into your hand!"

I have tried his method myself, in more than
one instance, and am inclined to think it is
founded on common-sense.

But in all our dealings with him, we should
remember that the horse's mouth is naturally
delicate and sensitive, though we so often find it
hardened by violence and ill-usage. The amount
of force we apply, therefore, whether small or
great, should be measured no less accurately than
the drops of laudanum administered to a patient
by the nurse. Reins are intended for the guidance
of the horse, not the support of his rider, and if
you do not feel secure without holding on by
something, rather than pluck at his mouth,
accept the ridicule of the position with its safety,
and grasp the mane!

Seriously, you may do worse in a difficulty, when your balance is in danger, and instinct prompts you to restore it, as, if a horse is struggling out of a bog, has dropped his hind legs in a brook, or otherwise come on his nose without actually falling, nothing so impedes his endeavours to right himself as a tug of the bridle at an inopportune moment. That instrument should be used for its legitimate purposes alone, and a strong seat in the saddle is the first essential for a light hand on the rein.

CHAPTER VI

SEAT

SOME people tell you they ride by "balance," others by "grip." I think a man might as well say he played the fiddle by "finger," or by ear. Surely in either case a combination of both is required to sustain the performance with harmony and success. The grip preserves the balance, which in turn prevents the grip becoming irksome. To depend on the one alone is to come home very often with a dirty coat, to cling wholly by the other is to court as much fatigue in a day as ought to serve for a week. I have more than once compared riding to swimming, it seems to require the same buoyancy of spirits, the same venture of body, the same happy combination of confidence, strength, and skill.

The seat a man finds easiest to himself, says the inimitable Mr. Jorrocks, "will in all humane probability be the easiest to his 'oss!" and in this, as in every other remark of the humorous grocer, there is no little wisdom and truth. "If he go smooth, *I am*,"[1] said a Frenchman, to whom a friend of mine offered a mount; "if he go rough, I shall not remain!" and doubtless the primary object of getting into a saddle, is to stay there at our own convenience, so long as circumstances permit.

But what a number of different attitudes do men adopt, in order to insure this permanent settlement. There is no position from the tongs in the fender, to the tailor on his shop-board, into which the equestrian has not forced his unaccustomed limbs, to avoid involuntary separation from his beast. The dragoon of fifty years ago was drilled to ride with a straight leg, and his foot barely resting on the stirrup, whereas the Oriental cavalry soldier, no mean proficient in the management of horse and weapon, tucks his knees up nearly to his chin, so that when he rises in the saddle, he towers above his little Arab as if he were standing rather than sitting on its back. The position, he argues, gives him a longer reach, and a stronger purchase for the use of sword and spear. If we are to judge by illuminated copies of Froissart, and other contemporary chronicles, it would seem that the armour-clad knight of the olden time, trusting in the depth and security of his saddle, *rode so long* as to derive no assistance whatever from his stirrups, sitting down on his

[1] *J'y suis.*

horse as much as possible, in dread, maybe, lest the point of an adversary's lance should hoist him fairly out of his place over a cantle six inches high, and send him clanging to the ground, in mail and plate, surcoat, helmet and plumes, with his lady - love, squires, yeomen, the marshals of the lists, and all his feudal enemies looking on!

Now the length of stirrup with which a man should ride, and in its adjustment consists much of the ease, grace, and security of his position, depends on the conformation of his lower limbs. If his thighs are long in proportion to his frame, flat and somewhat curved inwards, he will sit very comfortably at the exact length that raises him clear of his horse's withers, when he stands up in his stirrups with his feet home, and the majority of men thus limbed, on the majority of horses, will find this a good general rule. But when the legs are short and muscular, the thighs round and thick, the whole frame square and strong, more like wrestling than dancing, and many very superior riders are of this figure, the leathers must be pulled up a couple of holes and the foot thrust a little more forward, to obtain the necessary security of seat, at a certain sacrifice of grace and even ease. To look as neat as one can is a compliment to society; to be safe and comfortable is a duty to oneself.

Much also depends on the animal we bestride.

Horses low in the withers, and strong behind the saddle, particularly if inclined to "catch hold" a little, require in all cases rather shorter stirrups than their easier and truer-shaped stable-companions; nay, the varying roundness of barrel at different stages of condition affects the attitude of a rider, and most of us must have remarked, as horse and master get finer drawn towards the spring, how we let out the stirrups in proportion as we take in waistbelt and saddle-girths. Men rode well nevertheless, witness the Elgin Marbles, before the invention of this invaluable aid to horsemanship; and no equestrian can be considered perfect who is unable in a plunge or leap to stick on his horse bare-backed. Every boy should be taught to ride without stirrups, but not till he is tall and strong enough to grasp his pony firmly between his knees. A child of six or seven might injure itself in the effort, and ten, or eleven, is an early age enough for our young gentlemen to be initiated into the subtleties of the art. My own idea is that he should begin without reins, so as to acquire a seat totally independent of his hands, and should never be trusted with a bridle till it is perfectly immaterial to him whether he has hold of it or not. Neither should it be restored, after his stirrups have been taken away, till he has again proved himself independent of its support. When he has learned to canter round

Accept the ridicule, and grasp the mane!"

the school, and sit firm over a leaping-bar, with his feet swinging loose, and his hands in his pockets, he will have become a better horseman than ninety-nine out of every hundred who go out hunting. Henceforward you may trust him to take care of himself, and *swim alone*.

In every art it is well to begin from the very first with the best method ; and I would instil into a pupil, even of the tenderest years, that although his legs, and especially his knees, are to be applied firmly to his pony's sides, as affording a security against tumbling off, it is *from the loins* that he must really ride, when all is said and done.

I daresay most of us can remember the mechanical horse exhibited in Piccadilly some ten or twelve years ago, a German invention, remarkable for its ingenuity and the wonderful accuracy with which it imitated, in an exaggerated degree, the kicks, plunges, and other outrages practised by the most restive of the species to unseat their riders. Shaped in the truest symmetry, clad in a real horse's skin, with flowing mane and tail, this automaton represented the live animal in every particular, but for the pivot on which it turned, a shaft entering the belly below its girths, and communicating through the floor with the machinery that set in motion and regulated its astonishing vagaries. On mounting, the illusion was complete.

93

RIDING RECOLLECTIONS

Its very neck was so constructed with hinges that,
on pulling at the bridle, it gave you its head
without changing the direction of its body, exactly
like an unbroken colt as yet intractable to the bit.
At a word from the inventor, spoken in his own
language to his assistants below, this artificial
charger committed every kind of wickedness that
could be devised by a fiend in equine shape.   It
reared straight on end ; it lunged forward with its
nose between its fore feet, and its tail elevated to
a perpendicular, awkward and ungainly as that of
a swan *in reverse*.   It lay down on its side ; it
rose to its legs with a bounce, and finally, if the
rider's strength and dexterity enabled him still to
remain in the saddle, it wheeled round and round
with a velocity that could not fail at last to shoot
him out of his seat on to the floor, humanely
spread with mattresses, in anticipation of this
inevitable catastrophe.   It is needless to say how
such an exhibition drew, with so horse-loving a
public as our own.   No gentleman who fancied he
could "ride a bit" was satisfied till he had taken
his shilling's worth and the mechanical horse had
put him on his back.   But for the mattresses,
Piccadilly could have counted more broken collar-
bones than ever did Leicestershire in the blindest
and deepest of its Novembers.   Rough-riders
from the Life-Guards, Blues, Artillery, and half
the cavalry regiments in the service, came to try

conclusions with the spectre ; and, like antagonists of some automaton chess-player, retired defeated and dismayed.

For this universal failure, one could neither blame the men nor the military system taught in their schools. It stands to reason that human wind and muscle must sooner or later succumb to mechanical force. The inventor himself expressed surprise at the consummate horsemanship displayed by many of his fallen visitors, and admitted that more than one rough-rider would have tired out and subjugated any living creature of real flesh and blood ; while the essayists universally declared the imitation so perfect, that at no period of the struggle could they believe they were contending with clock-work, rather than the natural efforts of some wild unbroken colt.

But those who succeeded best, I remarked (and I speak with some little experience, having myself been indebted to the mattresses in my turn), were the horsemen who, allowing their loins to play freely, yielding more or less to every motion of the figure, did not trust exclusively for firmness of seat to the clasp of their knees and thighs. The mere balance-rider had not a chance ; the athlete who stuck on by main force found himself hurled into the air, with a violence proportioned to his own stubborn resistance ; but the artist who judiciously combined strength with skill, giving a little here that he might get a stronger purchase there, swaying his body loosely to meet and accompany every motion, while he kept his legs pressed hard against the saddle, withstood trick after trick and shock after shock creditably enough, till a hint muttered in German that it was time to displace him, put such mechanism in motion as settled the matter forthwith.

There was one detail, however, to be observed in the equipment of the mechanical horse that brings us to a question I have heard discussed amongst the best riders with very decided opinions on either side.

Formerly every saddle used to be made with padding about half an inch deep, sewn in the front rim of the flap against which a rider rests his knee, for the purpose, as it would seem, of affording him a stronger seat with its resistance and support.

Thirty or forty years ago a few noted sportsmen, despising such adventitious aid, began to adopt the open, or plain-flapped saddle; and, although not universal, it has now come into general use. It would certainly, of the two, have been the better adapted to the automaton I have described, as an inequality of surface was sadly in the way when the figure in its downward perpendicular, brought the rider's foot parallel with the point of its shoulders. The man's calf then necessarily slipped over the padding of his saddle, and it was impossible for him to get his leg back to its right place in time for a fresh outbreak when the model rose again to its proper level.

As I would prefer an open saddle for the artificial, so I do for the natural horse, and I will explain why.

I take it as a general and elementary rule, there is no better position for a rider than that which brings shoulder, hip, knee, and heel into one perpendicular line. A man thus placed on his horse cannot but sit well down with a bend in his back, and in this attitude, the one into which he would naturally fall, if riding at full speed, he has not only security of seat, but great command over the animal he bestrides. He will find, nevertheless, in crossing a country, or otherwise practising feats of horsemanship requiring the exercise of strength, that to get his knee an inch or two in advance of the correct line will afford such leverage as it were for the rest of his body as gives considerable advantage in any unusual difficulty, such as a drop-leap, for instance, with which he may have to contend. Now in the plain - flapped saddle, he can bend his leg as much as he likes, and put it indeed where he will.

This facility, too, is very useful in smuggling through a gap by a tree, often the most convenient egress, to make use of which, with a little skill and prudence, is a less hazardous experiment than it looks. A horse will take good care not to graze his own skin, and the space that admits of clearing his hips is wide enough for his rider's leg as well, if he hangs it over the animal's shoulder just where its neck is set on to the withers. But I would caution him to adopt this attitude carefully, and above all, in good time. He should take his foot out of the stirrup and make his preparatory arrangements some three or four strides off at least, so as to accommodate his change of seat to the horse's canter before rising at the leap, and if he can spare his hand nearest the tree, so as to "fend it off" a little at the same time, he will be surprised to find how safely and pleasantly he accomplished a transit through some awkward and dangerous fence.

But he must beware of delaying this little manœuvre till the last moment, when his horse is about to spring. It is then too late, and he will either find himself so thrown out of his seat as to lose balance and grip too, or will try to save his leg by shifting it back instead of forward, when much confusion, bad language, and perhaps a broken knee-pan will be the result.

Amongst other advantages of the open saddle we must not forget that it is cheaper by twenty shillings, and so sets off the shape of his forehand as to make a hunter look more valuable by twenty pounds.

SEAT

Nevertheless, it is still repudiated by some of our finest horsemen, who allege the sufficient reason that an inch or so of stuffing adds to their strength and security of seat. This, after all, is the *sine quâ non*, to which every article of equipment, even the important items of boots and breeches, should be subservient; and I may here remark that ease and freedom of dress are indispensable to a man who wishes to ride across a country not only in comfort, but in safety. I am convinced that tight, ill-fitting leathers may have broken bones to answer for. Many a good fellow comes down to breakfast stiff of gait, as if he were clothed in buckram, and can we wonder that he is hurt when, thus hampered and constrained, he falls stark and rigid, like a pasteboard policeman in a pantomime. ?

I have already protested against the solecism of saving yourself by the bridle. It is better, if you *must* have assistance, to follow the example of two or three notoriously fine riders and grasp the cantle of the saddle at the risk of breaking its tree. But in my humble opinion it is not well to be in the wrong even with Plato, and, notwithstanding these high authorities, we must consider such habits, however convenient on occasion, as errors in horsemanship. To a good rider the saddle ought to be a place of security as easy as an arm-chair.

RIDING RECOLLECTIONS

I have heard it asserted, usually by persons of lean and wiry frames, that with short legs and round thighs, it is impossible to acquire a firm seat on horseback; but in this, as in most matters of skill, I believe nature can be rendered obedient to education. Few men are so clumsily shaped but that they may learn to become strong and skilful riders if they will adopt a good system, and from the first resolve to sit *in the right place*; this, I think, should be in the very middle of the saddle, while bending the small of the back inwards, so that the weight of the body rests on that part of a horse's spine immediately behind his withers, under which his fore feet are placed, and on which, it has been ascertained, he can bear the heaviest load. When the animal stands perfectly still, or when it is extended at full speed, the most inexperienced horseman seems to fall naturally into the required position; but to preserve it, even through the regulated paces of the riding-school, demands constant effort and attention. The back-board is here, in my opinion, of great assistance to the beginner, as it forces him into an attitude that causes him to sit on the right part of his own person and his horse's back. It compels him also to carry his hands at a considerable distance off the horse's head, and thus entails also the desideratum of long reins.

The shortest and surest way, however, of

SEAT

attaining a firm seat on horseback is, after all, to practise without stirrups on every available opportunity. Many a valuable lesson may be taken while riding to covert and nobody but the student be a bit the wiser. Thus to trot and canter along, for two or three miles on end, is no bad training at the beginning of the season, and even an experienced horseman will be surprised to find how it gets him down in his saddle, and makes him feel as much at home there as he did in the previous March.

The late Captain Percy Williams, as brilliant a rider over a country as ever cheered a hound, and to whom few professional jockeys would have cared to give five pounds on a racecourse, assured me that he attributed to the above self-denying exercise that strength in the saddle which used to serve him so well from the distance home. When quartered at Hounslow with his regiment, the 9th Lancers, like other gay young light dragoons he liked to spend all his available time in London. There were no railroads in those days, and the coaches did not always suit for time ; but he owned a sound, speedy, high-trotting hack, and on this " bone-setter " he travelled backwards and forwards twelve miles of the great Bath Road, with military regularity, half as many times a week. He made it a rule to cross the stirrups over his horse's shoulders the moment he was off the stones at either end, only to be replaced when he reached his destination. In three months' time, he told me, he had gained more practical knowledge of horsemanship, and more muscular power below the waist, than in all the hunting, larking, and riding-school drill of the previous three years.

Grace is, after all, but the result of repressed strength. The loose and easy seat that seems to sway so carelessly with every motion, can tighten itself by instinct to the compression of a vice, and the "prettiest rider," as they say in Ireland, is probably the one whom a kicker or buck-jumper would find the most difficult to dislodge. No doubt in the field, the ride, the parade, or the polo-ground a strong seat is the first of those many qualities that constitute good horsemanship. The real adept is not to be unseated by any catastrophe less conclusive than complete downfall of man and beast; nay, even then he parts company without confusion, and it may be said of him as of "William of Deloraine," good at need in a like predicament—

> " Still sate the warrior, saddle fast,
>   Till, stumbling in the mortal shock,
>   Down went the steed, the girthing broke,
>   Hurled in a heap lay man and horse."

But I have a strong idea Sir William did not let his bridle go even then.

CHAPTER VII

VALOUR

" HE that would venture nothing must not get on horseback," says a Spanish proverb, and the same caution seems applicable to most manly amusements or pursuits. We cannot enter a boat, put on a pair of skates, take a gun in hand for covert shooting, or even run downstairs in a hurry without encountering risk ; but the amount of peril to which a horseman subjects himself seems proportioned inversely to the unconsciousness of it he displays.

"Where there is no fear there is no danger," though a somewhat reckless aphorism, is more applicable, I think, to the exercise of riding than to any other venture of neck and limbs. The horse is an animal of exceedingly nervous temperament, sympathetic too, in the highest degree, with the hand from which he takes his instructions. Its slightest vacillation affects him with electric rapidity, but from its steadiness he derives moral encouragement rather than physical support, and on those rare occasions when his own is insufficient, he seems to borrow daring and resolution from his rider.

If the man's heart is in the right place, his horse will seldom fail him ; and were we asked to name the one essential without which it is impossible to attain thorough proficiency in the saddle, we should not hesitate to say nerve.

Nerve, I repeat, in contradistinction to pluck. The latter takes us into a difficulty, the former brings us out of it. Both are comprised in the noble quality we call emphatically valour, but while the one is a brilliant and imposing costume, so is the other an honest wear-and-tear fabric, equally fit for all weathers, fine and foul.

"You shiver, Colonel—you are afraid," said an insubordinate Major, who ought to have been put under arrest then and there, to his commanding officer on the field of Prestonpans. "I *am* afraid, sir," answered the Colonel; "and if you were as much afraid as I am, *you would run away !*"

I have often thought this improbable anecdote exemplifies very clearly that most meritorious of all courage which asserts the dominion of our will over our senses. The Colonel's answer proves he was full of valour. He had lots of pluck, but, as he was bold enough to admit, a deficiency of nerve.

Now the field of Diana happily requires but a

VALOUR

slight percentage of daring and resolution compared with the field of Mars. I heard the late
Sir Francis Head, distinguished as a soldier, a
statesman, an author, and a sportsman, put the
matter in a few words, very tersely—and exceedingly to the point. "Under fire," said he, "there
is a guinea's-worth of danger, but it comes to you.
In the hunting-field, there is only three-ha'p'orth,
but *you go to it!*" In both cases, the courage
required is a mere question of degree, and as in
war, so in the chase, he is most likely to distinguish
himself whose daring, not to be dismayed, is
tempered with coolness, whose heart is always
stout and hopeful, while he never loses his
head.

Now as I understand the terms pluck and
nerve, I conceive the first to be a moral quality,
the result of education, sentiment, self-respect,
and certain high aspirations of the intellect; the
second, a gift of nature dependent on the health,
the circulation, and the liver. As memory to
imagination in the student, so is nerve to pluck
in the horseman. Not the more brilliant quality,
nor the more captivating, but sound, lasting,
available for all emergencies, and sure to conquer
in the long-run.

We will suppose two sportsmen are crossing a
country equally well mounted, and each full of
valour to the brim. A, to quote his admiring

friends, "has the pluck of the devil!" B, to use a favourite expression of the saddle-room, "has a good nerve." Both are bound to come to grief over some forbidding rails at a corner, the only way out, in the line hounds are running, and neither has any more idea of declining than had poor Lord Strathmore on a similar occasion when Jem Mason hallooed to him, "Eternal misery on this side, my lord, and certain death on the other!" So they harden their hearts, sit down in their saddles, and this is what happens :—

A's horse, injudiciously sent at the obstacle, *because* it is awkward, a turn too fast, slips in taking off, and strikes the top rail, which neither bends nor breaks, just below its knees. A flurried snatch at the bridle pulls its head in the air, and throws the animal skilfully to the ground at the moment it most requires perfect freedom for a desperate effort to keep on its legs. Rider and horse roll over in an "imperial crowner," and rise to their feet looking wildly about them, totally disconnected, and five or six yards apart.

This is not encouraging for B, who is obliged to follow, inasmuch as the place only offers room for one at a time, but as soon as his leader is out of the way, he comes steadily and quietly at the leap. His horse, too, slips in the tracks of its fallen comrade, but as it is going in a more collected form, it contrives to get its fore legs over the impediment, which catches it, however, inside the hocks, so that, balancing for a moment, it comes heavily on its nose. During these evolutions, B sits motionless in the saddle, giving the animal complete liberty of rein. An instinct of self-preservation and a good pair of shoulders turn the scale at the last moment, and although there is no denying they "had a squeak for it" in the scramble, B and his horse come off without a fall.

Now it was pluck that took both these riders into the difficulty, but nerve that extricated one of them without defeat.

I am not old enough to have seen the famous Mr. Assheton Smith in the hunting-field, but many of my early Leicestershire friends could remember him perfectly at his best, when he hunted that fine and formidable country, with the avowed determination, daily carried out, *of going into every field with his hounds !*

The expenditure of valour, for it really deserves the name, necessary to carry out such a style of riding can only be appreciated by those who have tried to keep in a good place during thirty or forty minutes, over any part of the Quorn and Cottesmore counties lying within six miles of Billesdon. Where should we be but for the gates ? I think I may answer, neither there nor thereabouts ! I have reason to believe the many stories told of "Tom Smith's" skill and daring are little, if at all, exaggerated. He seems admitted by all to have been the boldest, as he was one of the best, horsemen that ever got into a saddle with a hunting-whip in his hand.

Though subsequently a man of enormous wealth, in the prime of life he lived on the allowance, adequate but not extravagant, made him by his father, and did by no means give those high prices for horses, which, on the principle that "money makes the mare to go," are believed by many sportsmen to ensure a place in the front rank. He entertained no fancies as to size, action, above all, peculiarities in mouths and tempers. Little or big, sulky, violent, or restive, if a horse could gallop and jump, he was a hunter the moment he found himself between the legs of Tom Smith.

There is a namesake of his hunting at present from Melton, who seems to have taken several leaves out of his book. Captain Arthur Smith, with every advantage of weight, nerve, skill, seat, and hand, is never away from the hounds. Moreover, he always likes his horse, and his horse always seems to like him. This gentleman, too, is blessed with an imperturbable temper, which I have been given to understand the squire of Tedworth was *not*.

Instances of Tom Smith's daring are endless.

VALOUR

How characteristic was his request to a farmer
near Glengorse, that he would construct such a
fence as should effectually prevent the field from
getting away in too close proximity to his hounds.
" I can make you up a stopper," said the good-
natured yeoman, "and welcome ; but what be
you to do yourself, Squire, for I know you like
well to be with 'em when they run ? "

"Never mind me," was the answer ; "you do
what I ask you.   I never saw a fence in this
country I couldn't get over *with a fall !* " and,
sure enough, the first day the hounds found a fox
in that well-known covert, Tom Smith was seen
striding along in the wake of his darlings, having
tumbled neck-and-crop over the obstacle he had
demanded, in perfect good-humour and content.

If valour, then, is a combination of pluck and
nerve, he may be called the most valorous
sportsman that ever got upon a horse, while
affording another example of the partiality with
which fortune favours the bold, for although he
has had between eighty and ninety falls in a
season, he was never really hurt, I believe, but
once in his life.

"That is a *brave* man !" I have heard Lord
Gardner say in good-humoured derision, pointing
to some adventurous sportsman, whose daring so
far exceeded his dexterity as to bring horse and
rider into trouble ; but his lordship's own nerve

was so undeniable, that like many others he may have undervalued a quality of which he could not comprehend the want.

Most hunting men, I fancy, will agree with me, that of all obstacles we meet with in crossing a country, timber draws most largely on the reserve fund of courage hoarded away in that part of a hero's heart which is nearest his mouth. The highest rails I ever saw attempted were ridden at by Lord Gardner some years ago, while out with Mr. Tailby's hounds near the Ram's Head. With a fair holding scent, and the pack bustling their fox along over the grass, there was no time for measurement, but I remember perfectly well that being in the same field, some fifty yards behind him, and casting longing looks at the fence, totally impracticable in every part, I felt satisfied the corner he made for was simply an impossibility.

"We had better turn round and go home!" I muttered in my despair.

The leap consisted of four strong rails, higher than a horse's withers, an approach downhill, a take-off poached by cattle, and a landing into a deep muddy lane. I can recall at this moment the beautiful style in which my leader brought his horse to its effort. Very strong in the saddle, with the finest hands in the world, leaning far back, and sitting well down, he seemed to rouse as it were, and concentrate the energies of the

VALOUR

animal for its last half-stride, when, rearing itself almost perpendicularly, it contrived to get safe over, only breaking the top rail with a hind leg.

This must have lowered the leap by at least a foot, yet when I came to it, thus reduced, and "made easy," it was still a formidable obstacle, and I felt thankful to be on a good jumper.

Of late years I have seen Mr. Powell, who is usually very well mounted, ride over exceedingly high and forbidding timber so persistently, as to have earned from that material, the *nom de chasse* by which he is known amongst his friends.

But perhaps the late Lord Cardigan, the last of the Brudenells, afforded in the hunting-field, as in all other scenes of life, the most striking example of that "pluck" which is totally independent of youth, health, strength, or any other physical advantage. The courage that in advanced middle-age governed the steady manœuvres of Bulganak, and led the death-ride at Balaclava, burned bright and fierce to the end. The graceful seat might be less firm, the tall soldierlike figure less upright, but Mars, one of his last and best hunters, was urged to charge wood and water by the same bold heart at seventy, that tumbled Langar into the Uppingham road over the highest gate in Leicestershire at twenty-six. The foundation of Lord Cardigan's whole character was valour. He loved it, he prized it, he admired it in others, he was conscious and proud of it in himself.

So jealous was he of this chivalrous quality, that even in such a matter of mere amusement as riding across a country, he seemed to attach some vague sense of disgrace to the avoidance of a leap, however dangerous, if hounds were running at the time, and was notorious for the recklessness with which he would plunge into the deepest rivers though he could not swim a stroke!

This I think is to court *real* danger for no sufficient object.

Lord Wolverton, than whom no man has ridden straighter and more enthusiastically to hounds, ever since he left Oxford, once crossed the Thames in this most perilous fashion,—for he too has never learnt to swim—during a run with "the Queen's." "But," said I, protesting subsequently against such hardihood, "you were risking your life at every stroke."

"I never thought of that," was the answer, "till I got safe over, and it was no use bothering about it then."

Lord Cardigan, however, seemed well aware of his danger, and, in my own recollection, had two very narrow escapes from drowning in these uncalled-for exploits.

The gallant old cavalry officer's death was in

keeping with his whole career. At threescore years and ten he insisted on mounting a dangerous animal that he would not have permitted any friend to ride. What happened is still a mystery. The horse came home without him, and he never spoke again, though he lived till the following day.

But these are sad reflections for so cheerful a subject as daring in the saddle. Red is our colour, not black, and, happily, in the sport we love, there are few casualties calling forth more valour than is required to sustain a bloody nose, a broken collar-bone, or a sound ducking in a wet ditch. Yet it is extraordinary how many good fellows riding good horses find themselves defeated in a gallop after hounds, from indecision and uncertainty, rather than want of courage, when the emergency actually arises. Though the danger, according to Sir Francis Head, is about a hap'orth, it might possibly be valued at a penny, and nobody wants to discover, in his own person, the exact amount. Therefore are the chivalry of the Midland Counties to be seen on occasion panic-stricken at the downfall or disappearance of a leader. And a dozen feet of dirty water will wholly scatter a field of horsemen who would confront an enemy's fire without the quiver of an eyelash. Except timber, of which the risk is obvious at a glance, nothing frightens the *half*-hard, so much as a brook. It is difficult, you see, to please them, the uncertainty of the limpid impediment being little less forbidding than the certainty of the stiff!

But it does require dash and coolness, pluck and nerve, a certain spice of something that may fairly be called valour, to charge cheerfully at a brook when we have no means of ascertaining its width, its depth, or the soundness of its banks. Horses, too, are apt to share the misgivings of their riders, and water-jumping, like a loan to a poor relation, if not done freely, had better not be done at all.

The fox, and consequently the hounds, as we know, will usually cross at the narrowest place, but even if we can mark the exact spot, fences, or the nature of the ground, may prevent our getting there. What are we to do? If we follow a leader, and he drops short, we are irretrievably defeated; if we make our own selection, the gulf may be as wide as the Thames. "Send him at it!" says valour, "and take your chance!" Perhaps it is the best plan after all. There is something in luck, a good deal in the reach of a horse's stride at a gallop, and if we *do* get over, we *rather* flatter ourselves for the next mile or two that we have "done the trick!"

To enter on the subject of "hard riding," as it

is called, without honourable mention of the habit and the side-saddle, would in these days betray both want of observation and politeness; but ladies, though they seem to court danger no less freely than admiration, possess, I think, as a general rule, more pluck than nerve. I can recall an instance very lately, however, in which I saw displayed by one of the gentlest of her sex, an amount of courage, coolness, and self-possession that would have done credit to a hero. This lady, who had not quite succeeded in clearing a high post-and-rail with a boggy ditch on the landing side, was down and under her horse. The animal's whole weight rested on her legs, so as to keep her in such a position, that her head lay between its fore and hind feet, where the least attempt at a struggle, hemmed in by those four shining shoes, must have dashed her brains out. She seemed in no way concerned for her beauty, or her life, but gave judicious directions to those who rescued her as calmly and courteously as if she had been pouring out their tea.

The horse, though in that there is nothing unusual, behaved like an angel, and the fair rider was extricated without very serious injury; but I thought to myself, as I remounted and rode on, that if a legion of Amazons could be rendered amenable to discipline they would conquer the world.

RIDING RECOLLECTIONS

No man, till he has tried the experiment, can conceive how awkward and powerless one feels in a lady's seat. They themselves affirm that with the crutch, or second pommel on the near side, they are more secure than ourselves ; but when I see those delicate, fragile forms flying over wood and water, poised on precipitous banks, above all crashing through strong bullfinches, I am struck with admiration at the mysteries of nature, among which not the least wonderful seems the feminine desire to excel. And they *do* excel when resolved they will, even in those sports and exercises which seem more naturally belonging to the masculine department. It was but the other day, a boat-man in the Channel told me he saw a lady swimming alone more than half a mile off shore. Now that the universal rink has brought skating into fashion, the "many-twinkling feet," that smoothest glide and turn most deftly, are shod with such dainty boots as never could be worn by the clumsier sex. At lawn-tennis the winning service is offered by some seductive hoyden in her teens ; and, although in the game of cricket the Graces have as yet been males, at no distant day we may expect to see the best batsman at the Oval bowled out, or perhaps caught, by a woman !

Yes, the race is in the ascendant. It takes the heaviest fish—I mean *real* fish—with a rod and line. It kills its grouse right and left—in the

Breaking the top rail with a hind leg

moor among the heather.   It shoulders a rifle no
heavier than a pea-shooter, but levels the toy so
straight that, after some cunning stalk, a "stag of
ten" goes down before the white hand and taper
finger, as becomes his antlers and his sex.   Lastly,
when it gets upon Bachelor, or Benedict, or
Othello, or any other high-flyer with a suggestive
name, it sails away close, often too close, to the
hounds, leaving brothers, husbands, even admirers,
hopelessly in the rear.

Now, I hope I am not going to express a
sentiment that will offend their prejudices, and
cause young women to call me an old one, but I
do consider that in these days ladies who go out
hunting *ride a turn too hard*.   Far be it from me to
assert that the field is no place for the fair ; on the
contrary, I hold that their presence adds in every
respect to its charms.   Neither would I protest
against their jumping, and relegate them to the
bridle-roads or lanes.   Nothing of the kind.   Let
the greatest care be taken in the selection of their
horses ; let their saddles and bridles be fitted to
such a nicety that sore backs and sore mouths are
equally impossible, and let trustworthy servants
be told off to attend them during the day.   Then,
with everything in their favour, over a fair country,
fairly fenced, why should they not ride on and
take their pleasure ?

But even if their souls disdain to follow a

regular pilot (and I may observe his office requires no little nerve, as they are pretty quick on to a leader if he gets down), I would entreat them not to try "cutting out the work," as it is called, but rather to wait and see one rider, at least, over a leap before they attempt it themselves. It is frightful to think of a woman landing in a pit, a water-course, or even so deep a ditch as may cause the horse to roll over her when he falls. With her less muscular frame she is more easily injured than a man; with her finer organisation she cannot sustain injury as well. It turns one sick to think of her dainty head between a horse's hind legs, or of those cruel pommels bruising her delicate ribs and bosom. It is at least twenty to one in *our* favour every time we fall, whereas with her the odds are all the other way, and it is almost twenty to one she must be hurt.

What said the wisest of kings concerning a fair woman without discretion? We want no Solomon to remind us that with her courage roused, her ambition excited, all the rivalry of her nature called into play, she has nowhere more need of this judicious quality than in the hunting-field.

CHAPTER VIII

DISCRETION

IT has been called the better part of valour, and doubtless, when wanting, the latter is as likely to sustain irretrievable reverses as a ship without a rudder, or a horse without a bridle. The two should always travel together; but it appears to me that we meet the cautious brother most frequently on our journey through life.

In the chase, however, they seem to share their presence impartially enough. Valour is very much to the front at the covert side, and shows again with great certainty after dinner; but discretion becomes paramount and almost ubiquitous when the hounds run, being called on indeed to act for us in every field. Sometimes, particularly when countries are blind early in November, we abandon ourselves so entirely to its guidance as little by little to lose all our self-reliance, till at last we feel comfortable nowhere but in the high road; and most of us, I daresay, can recall occasions on which we have been so

RIDING RECOLLECTIONS

utterly discomfited by an early disappointment (in plain English, a fence we were afraid to jump) as to give in without an effort, although the slightest dash of valour at the right moment would have carried us triumphantly out of defeat.

Never mind. Like a French friend of mine, who expresses his disinclination to our *chasse au renard* by protesting, "*Monsieur, je ne cherche pas mes émotions à me casser le cou*," when we are avowedly in pursuit of pleasure we ought to take it exactly as suits us best. There are two ends of the string in every run with hounds. Wisdom pervades each of these, but eschews the various gradations between. In front rides valour with discretion; in rear, discretion without valour; and in the middle a tumultuous throng, amongst whom neither quality is to be recognised. With too little of the one to fly, not enough of the other to creep, they waver at the fences, hurry at the gaps, get in each other's way at the gates, and altogether make exceedingly slow progress compared to their efforts and their excitement.

Valour without discretion, I had almost forgotten to observe, was down and under his horse at the first difficulty.

We will let the apex of the pyramid alone for the present, taking the safest and broadest end of the hunt first.

DISCRETION

If, then, you have achieved so bad a start that it is impossible to make up your lee-way, or if you are on a hack with neither power nor intention to ride in the front rank, be sure you cannot take matters too coolly should you wish to command the line of chase and see as much as possible of the fun.

I am supposing the hounds have found a good fox that knows more than one parish, and are running him with a holding scent. However favourable your start, and fate is sure to arrange a good one for a man too badly mounted to avail himself of it, let nothing induce you to keep near the pack. At a mile off you can survey and anticipate their general direction, at a quarter that distance you must ride every turn. Do not be disordered by the brilliancy of the pace should their fox go straight up wind. If he does not sink it within five minutes he means reaching a drain, and another five will bring the "who-whoop!" that marks him to ground. This is an unfailing deduction, but happily the most discreet of us are apt to forget it. Time after time we are so fooled by the excitement of our gallop that even experience does not make us wise, and we enjoy the scurry, exclaiming, "What a pity!" when it is over, as if we had never been out hunting before. It would be useless to distress your hack for so short a spin, rather keep wide of the line, if possible, on high ground, and calculate by the wind, the coverts, and the general aspect of the country, where a fox is most likely to make his point.

I have known good runs in the Shires seen fairly, from end to end, by a lady in a waggonette.

When business really begins, men are apt to express in various ways their intention of taking part. Some use their eyes, some their heels, and some their flasks. Do you trust your brains, they will stand you in better stead than spurs, or spectacles, or even brandy diluted with curaçoa. Keep your attention fixed on the chase, watch the pack as long as you can, and when those white specks have vanished into space, depend on your own skill in woodcraft and knowledge of country to bring you up with them again. Above all, while they are actually in motion, distrust the bobbing hats and spots of scarlet that you mark in a distant cluster behind the hedge. What are they but the field? and the field, if it is *really* a run, are pretty sure to be *out of it*.

The first flight you will find very difficult to keep in view. At the most it consists of six or seven horsemen riding fifty or a hundred yards apart, and even its followers become so scattered and detached that in anything like an undulating country they are completely hidden from observation. If you *do* catch a glimpse of them, how

DISCRETION

slow they seem to travel! and yet, when you nick in presently, heaving flanks, red faces, and excited voices will tell a very different tale.

Trotting soberly along, then, with ears and eyes wide open, carefully keeping down wind, not only because the hounds are sure to bend in that direction, but also that you can thus hear before you see them, and take measures accordingly, you will have ridden very few miles before you are gladdened by the cheerful music of the pack, or more probably a twang from the horn. The scent is rarely so good as to admit of hounds running for thirty or forty minutes without a check; indeed, on most days they are likely to be at fault more than once during the lapse of half an hour, when the huntsman's science will be required to cast them, and, in some cases, to assist them in losing their fox. Now is your time to press on with the still undefeated hack. If you are wise, you will not leave the lanes to which I give you the credit of having stuck religiously from the start. At least, do not think of entering a field unless the track of an obvious bridle-road leads safely into the next.

A man who never jumps at all can by no possibility be "pounded," whereas the easiest and safest of gaps into an enclosure may mean a bullfinch with two ditches at the other end.

Perhaps you will find yourself ahead of everyone

as the hounds spread, and stoop and dash forward
with a whimper that makes the sweetest of music
in your ears.   Perhaps, as they swarm across the
very lane in which you are standing, discretion
may calmly open the gate for valour, who curses
him in his heart, wondering what business he has
to be there at all.

There is jealousy even in the hunting-field,
though we prefer to call it keenness, emulation, a
fancy for riding our own line, and I fear that with
most of us, in spite of the kindly sympathies and
joyous expansion of the chase, "*ego et præterea
nihil*" is the unit about which our aspirations
chiefly revolve.

"What is the use?" I once heard a plaintive
voice lamenting behind a blackthorn, while the
hounds were baying over a drain at the finish of
a clipping thirty minutes on the grass.   "I've
spoilt my hat, I've torn my coat, I've lamed my
horse, I've had two falls, I went first, I'll take my
oath, from end to end, and there's that d—d
fellow on the coffee-coloured pony gets here
before me after all!"

There are times, no doubt, when valour must
needs yield the palm to discretion.

Let us see how this last respectable quality
serves us at the other and nobler extremity of the
hunt, for it is there, after all, that our ambition
points, and our wishes chiefly tend.

DISCRETION

"Are you a hard rider?" asked an inquiring lady of Mr. Jorrocks.

"The hardest in England," answered that facetious worthy, adding to himself, "I may say that, for I never goes off the 'ard road if I can help it."

Now, instead of following so cautious an example, let us rather cast overboard a superfluity of discretion, that would debar us the post of honour we are fain to occupy, retaining only such a leavening of its virtue as will steer us safely between the two extremes. While the hounds are racing before us, with a good scent, in an open country, let our gallant hunter be freely urged by valour to the front, while at the same time discretion holds him hard by the head, lest a too inconsiderate daring should endanger his rider's neck.

If a man has the luck to be on a good timber-jumper, now is the time to take advantage freely of its confidential resources. If not pulled about, and interfered with, a hunter that understands his business leaps this kind of fence, so long as he is fresh, with ease to himself and security to his rider. He sees exactly what he has to do, and need not rise an inch higher, nor fling himself an inch farther than is absolutely necessary, whereas a hedge induces him to make such exertions as may cover the uncertainty it conceals. But, on the other hand, the binder will usually bear tampering with, which the bar will *not*, therefore *if* your own courage and your horse's skill tempt you to negotiate rails, stiles, or even a gate—and this last is *very* good form—sound discretion warns you to select the first ten or fifteen minutes of a run for such exhibitions, but to avoid them religiously when the deep ground and the pace have begun to tell.

Assheton Smith himself, though he scouted the idea of ever turning from anything, had in so far the instinct of self-preservation, that when he thought his horse likely to fall over such an obstacle, he put him at it somewhat *a-slant*, so that the animal should get at least one fore leg clear, and tumble on to its side, when this accomplished rider was pretty sure to rise unhurt with the reins in his hand.

Now this diagonal style of jumping, judiciously practised, is not without its advantages at less dangerous fences than the uncompromising bit of timber that turns us over. It necessarily increases the width of a bank, affording the horse more room for foothold, as it decreases the height and strength of the growers, by taking them the way they lie, and may, on occasion, save a good hunter from a broken back, the penalty for dropping both hind legs simultaneously and perpendicularly into some steep cut ditch he has failed to cover in his stride.

DISCRETION

Discretion, you observe, should accompany the hardest riders, and is not to be laid aside even in the confusion and excitement of a fall.

This must prove a frequent casualty with every man, however well mounted, if the hounds show sport and he means to be with them while they run. It seems a paradox, but the oftener you are down, the less likely you are to be hurt. Practice soon teaches you to preserve presence of mind, or, as I may be allowed to call it, discretion, and when you know exactly where your horse is, you can get away from him before he crushes you with the weight of his body. A foot or a hand thrust out at the happy moment, is enough to "fend you off," and your own person seldom comes to the ground with such force as to do you any harm, if there is plenty of dirt. In the absence of that essential to sport, hunters are not distressed, and therefore do not often fall.

If, however, you have undertaken to temper the rashness of a young one with your own discretion, you must expect occasional reverses; but even thus, there are many chances in your favour, not the least of which is your pupil's elasticity. Lithe and agile, he will make such gallant efforts to save himself as usually obviate the worst consequences of his mistake. The worn-out, the underbred, or the distressed horse comes down like a lump of lead, and neither

K   127

valour nor discretion are much help to us then.

From the pace at which hounds cross a country, there is unfortunately no time to practise that most discreet manœuvre called "leading over," when the fence is of so formidable a nature as to threaten certain discomfiture, yet I have seen a few tall, powerful, active men, spring off and on their horses with such rapidity as to perform this feat successfully in all the hurry of a burst. The late Colonel Wyndham, who, when he commanded the Greys, in which regiment he served at Waterloo, was said by George the Fourth to be the handsomest man in the army, possessed with a giant's stature the pliant agility of a harlequin. A finer rider never got into a saddle. Weighing nineteen stone, I have seen him in a burst across Leicestershire, go for twenty minutes with the best of the light-weights, occasionally relieving his horse by throwing himself off, leaping a fence alongside of it, and vaulting on again, without checking the animal sufficiently to break its stride.

The lamented Lord Mayo, too, whose tall stalwart frame was in keeping with those intellectual powers that India still recalls in melancholy pride, was accustomed, on occasion, thus to surmount an obstacle, no less successfully among the bullfinches of Northamptonshire than the banks and ditches of Kildare. Perhaps the best

DISCRETION

rider of his family, and it is a bold assertion, for when five or six of the brothers are out hunting, there will always be that number of tall heavy men, answering to the name of Bourke in the same field with the hounds, Lord Mayo, or rather Lord Naas (for the best of his sporting career closed with his succession to the earldom), was no less distinguished for his daring horsemanship, than his tact in managing a country, and his skill in hunting a pack of hounds. That he showed less forethought in risking a valuable life than in conducting the government of an empire, we must attribute to his personal courage and keen delight in the chase, but that he humorously deplored the scarcity of discretion amongst its votaries, the following anecdote, as I had it from himself, sufficiently attests.

While he hunted his own hounds in Kildare, his most constant attendant, though on foot, was a nondescript character, such as is called "a tight boy" in Ireland, and nowhere else, belonging to a class that never seem to do a day's work, nor to eat a plentiful meal, but are always pleasant, obliging, idle, hungry, thirsty, and supremely happy. Running ten miles on foot to covert, Mick, as he was called, would never leave the hounds till they reached their kennels at night. Thus, plodding home one evening by his lordship's horse, after an unusually long and fatiguing run, the rider could not help expostulating with the walker on such a perverse misapplication of strength, energy, and perseverance. "Why, look at the work you have been doing," said his lordship; "with a quarter of the labour you might have earned three or four shillings at least. What a fool you must be, Mick, to neglect your business, and lose half your potatoes, that you may come out with my hounds!"

Mick reflected a moment, and looked up. "Ah! me lard," replied he, with such a glance of fun as twinkles nowhere but in the Irish blue of an Irish eye, "it's truth your lardship's spakin' this night; *av there was no fools, there'd be sorra few fox-hunters!*"

Let us return to the question of discretion, and how we are to combine it with an amusement that makes fools of us all.

While valour, then, bids us take our fences as they come, discretion teaches us that each should be accomplished in the manner most suitable to its peculiar requirements. When a bank offers foothold, and we see the possibility of dividing a large leap by two, we should pull back to a trot, and give our horse a hint that he will do well to spring on and off the obstacle in accordance with a motion of our hand. If, on the contrary, his effort must be made at a black and forbidding bullfinch, with the chance of a wide ditch, or even

"I've spoilt my hat, I've torn my coat"

DISCRETION

a tough ashen rail, beyond, it is wise, should we mean having it at all, to catch hold of the bridle and increase our pace, for the last two or three strides, with such energy as shall shoot us through the thorns like a harlequin through a trap-door, leaving the orifice to close up behind, with no more traces of our transit than are left by a bird!

Perhaps we find an easy place under a tree, with an overhanging branch, and sidle daintily up to it, bending the body and lowering the head as we creep through, to the admiration of an indiscreet friend on a rash horse, who spoils a good hat and utters an evil execration while trying to follow our example. Or it may be, rejoicing to find ourselves on arable land, that actually rides light and yet carries a scent,

> " Solid and tall,
> The rasping wall,"

challenges us a quarter of a mile off to face it or go home, for it offers neither gate nor gap, and seems to meet the sky-line on either side. I do not know whether others are open to the same deception, but to my own eye, a wall appears more, and a hedge less, than its real height at a certain distance off. The former, however, is a most satisfactory leap when skilfully accomplished, and not half so arduous as it looks.

" Have it!" says valour. " Yes, but very

slow," replies discretion. And, sure enough, we calm the free, generous horse into a trot, causing him to put his very nose over the obstacle before taking off; when bucking into the air, like a deer, he leaves it behind him with little more effort than a girl puts to her skipping-rope. The height an experienced wall-jumper will clear seems scarcely credible. A fence of this description, which measurement proves to be fully six feet, was jumped by the well-known Colonel Miles three or four years ago in the Badminton country without displacing a stone, and although the rider's consummate horsemanship afforded every chance of success, great credit is due to the good hunter that could make such an effort with so heavy a man on its back.

The knack of wall-jumping, however, is soon learned even by the most inexperienced animals, and I may here observe that I have often been surprised at the discretion shown by young horses, when ridden close to hounds, in negotiating fences requiring sagacity and common-sense. I am aware that my opinion is singular, and I only give it as the result, perhaps exceptional, of my own limited experience; but I must admit that I have been carried by a pupil, on his first day, over awkward places, up and down banks, in and out of ravines, or under trees, with a docility and circumspection I have looked for from the veterans

DISCRETION

in vain. Perhaps the old horse knows me as well as I know him, and thinks also that he knows best. I am bound to say he never fails me when I trust him, but he likes his head let alone, and insists on having it all his own way. When his blood is really up, and the hero of a hundred fights considers it worth while to put forth his strength, I am persuaded he is even bolder than his junior.

Not only at the fences, however, do we require discretion. There is a right way and a wrong of traversing every acre of ground that lies between them. On the grass, we must avoid crossing high ridge-and-furrow in a direct line; rather let us take it obliquely, or, if the field be not too large, go all the way round by the headland. For an unaccustomed horse there is nothing so trying as those up-and-down efforts, that resemble the lurches of a boat in a heavy sea. A very true-shaped animal will learn to glide smoothly over them after a season or two, but these inequalities of surface must always be a tax on wind and muscular powers at best. The easiest goer in ridge-and-furrow that we have yet seen is a fox. Surely no other quadruped has nature gifted with so much strength and symmetry in so small a compass.

Amongst the ploughs, though the fences are happily easier, forethought and consideration are even more required for ground. After much rain, do not enter a turnip-field if you can help it, the large, frequent roots loosen the soil, and your horse will go in up to his hocks; young wheat also it is well to avoid, if only for reasons purely selfish; but on the fallows, when you find a *wet* furrow, lying the right way, put on steam, splash boldly ahead, and never leave it so long as it serves you in your line. The same may be said of a footpath, even though its guidance should entail the jumping of half a dozen stiles. Sound foothold reduces the size of any leap, and while you are travelling easily above the ground, the rest of the chase, fox and hounds too, as well as horses, though in a less degree, are labouring through the mire.

When your course is intersected by narrow water-cuts, for purposes of irrigation, by covered drains, or deep, grass-grown cart-ruts, it will be well to traverse them obliquely, so that, if they catch the stride of his gallop, your horse may only get one foot in at a time. He will then right himself with a flounder, whereas, if held by both legs, either before or behind, the result is a rattling fall, very dangerous to his back in the one case, and to your own neck in the other.

Valour of course insists that a hunter should do what he is bid, but there are some situations

DISCRETION

in which the beast's discretion pleads reasonably
enough for some forbearance from its master. If
a good horse, thoroughly experienced in the
exigencies of the sport, that you have ridden a
season or two, and flatter yourself you understand,
persistently refuses a fence, depend upon it there
is sufficient reason. The animal may be lame
from an injury just received, may have displaced
a joint, broken a tendon, or even ruptured an
artery. Perhaps it is so blown as to feel it must
fall in the effort you require. At any rate do not
persevere. Horses have been killed, and men
also, through a sentiment of sheer obstinacy that
would not be denied, and humanity should at
least think shame to be outdone in discretion by
the brute. A horse is a wise creature enough,
or he could never carry us pleasantly to hounds.
An old friend of mine used to say, " People
talk about size and shape, shoulders, quarters,
blood, bone, and muscle, but for my part, give
me a hunter with brains. He has to take care
of the biggest fool of the two, and think for
both ! "

Discretion, then, is one of the most valuable
qualities for an animal charged with such heavy
responsibilities, that bears us happy and triumphant during the day, and brings us safe home at
night. Who would grudge a journey across St.
George's Channel to find this desirable quality

in its highest perfection at Ballinasloe or Cahirmee? for indeed it is not too much to say, that whatever we may think of her natives, the most discreet and sagacious of our hunters come over from the Emerald Isle.

CHAPTER IX

IRISH HUNTERS

" AN' niver laid an iron to the sod!" was a
metaphor I once heard used by an
excellent fellow from Limerick, to convey the
brilliant manner in which a certain four-year-old
he was describing performed during a burst,
when, his owner told me, he went clean away
from all rivals in his gallop, and flew every wall,
bank, and ditch in his stride.

The expression, translated into English, would
seem to imply that he neither perched on the
grass-grown banks, with all four feet at once, like
a cat, nor struck back at them with his hind legs,
like a dog; and perhaps my friend made the
more account of this hazardous style of jumping, that it seemed so foreign to the usual
characteristics of the Irish horse.

For those who have never hunted in Ireland,
I must explain that the country as a general rule
is fenced on a primitive system, requiring little
expenditure or capital beyond the labour of a

man, or, as he is there called, "a boy," with a
short pipe in his mouth and a spade in his hand.
The light-hearted operative, gay, generous, reckless, high-spirited, and by no means a free worker,
simply throws a bank up with the soil that he
scoops out of the ditch, reversing the process,
and filling the latter by levelling the former,
when a passage is required for carts, or cattle,
from one enclosure to the next. I ought nevertheless to observe, that many landlords, with a
munificence for which I am at a loss to account,
go to the expense of erecting massive pillars of
stone, ostensibly gate - posts, at commanding
points, between which supports, however, they
seldom seem to hang a gate, though it is but
justice to admit that when they do, the article is
usually of iron, very high, very heavy, and
fastened with a strong padlock, though its object
seems less apparent, when we detect within
convenient distance on either side a gap through
which one might safely drive a gig.

It is obvious, then, that this kind of fence, at
its widest and deepest, requires considerable
activity as well as circumspection on a horse's
part, and forbearance in handling on that of a
rider. The animal must gather itself to spring
like a goat, on the crest of the eminence it has
to surmount, with perfect liberty of head and
neck, for the climb, and subsequent effort, that

may or may not be demanded. Neither man
nor beast can foresee what is prepared for them
on the landing side, and a clever Irish hunter
brings itself up short in an instant, should the
gulf be too formidable for its powers, balancing
on the brink, to look for a better spot, or even
leaping back again into the field from which it
came.

That the Irishman rides with a light bridle and
lets it very much alone is the necessary result.
His pace at the fences must be slow, because it
is not a horse's nature, however rash, to rush at
a place like the side of a house; and instinct
prompts the animal to collect itself without
restraint from a rider's hand, while any inter-
ference during the second and downward spring
would only tend to pull it back into the chasm
it is doing its best to clear.

The efforts by which an Irish hunter surmounts
these national impediments is like that of a hound
jumping a wall. The horse leaps to the top with
fore and hind feet together, where it dwells, almost
imperceptibly, while shifting the purchase, or
"changing," as the natives call it, in the shortest
possible stride, of a few inches at most, to make
the second spring. Every good English hunter
will strike back with his hind legs when surprised
into sudden exertion, but only a proficient bred,
or at least taught, in the sister island, can master

the feat described above in such artistic form as leads one to believe that, like Pegasus, the creature has wings at every heel. No man who has followed hounds in Meath, Kilkenny, or Kildare will ever forget the first time, when, to use the vernacular of those delightful countries, he rode "an accomplished hunter over an intricate lep!"

But the merit is not heaven - born. On the contrary, it seems the result of patient and judicious tuition, called by Irish breakers "training," in which they show much knowledge of character and sound common-sense.

In some counties, such as Roscommon and Connemara, the brood mare indeed, with the foal at her foot, runs wild over extensive districts, and, finding no gates against which to lean, leaps leisurely from pasture to pasture, pausing, perhaps, in her transit to crop the sweeter herbage from some bank on which she is perched. Where mamma goes her little one dutifully follows, imitating the maternal motions, and as a charming mother almost always has a charming daughter, so, from its earliest foalhood, the future hunter acquires an activity, courage, and sagacity that shall hereafter become the admiration of crowded hunting-fields in the land of the Saxon far, far away!

But whereas in many parts of Ireland improved

agriculture denies space for the unrestrained
vagaries of these early lessons, a judicious system
is adopted that substitutes artificial education for
that of nature. "It is wonderful we don't get
more falls," said one of the boldest and best of
lady riders, who during many seasons followed
the pilotage of Jem Mason, and but for failing
eyesight, could sometimes have gone before
him, "when we consider that we all ride half-
broken horses," and, no doubt, on our side of the
Channel, the observation contained a great deal
of truth. But in this respect our neighbours
show more wisdom. They seldom bring a pupil
into the hunting-field till the elementary discipline
has been gone through that teaches him when he
comes to his fence *what to do with it.* He may
be three, he may be four. I have seen a sportsman in Kilkenny so unassumingly equipped that
instead of boots he wore wisps of straw called, I
believe, *sooghauns*, go in front for a quarter of an
hour on a two-year-old! Whatever his age, the
colt shows himself an experienced hunter when
it is necessary to leap. Not yet *mouthed*, with
unformed paces and wandering action, he may
seem the merest baby on the road or across a
field, but no veteran can be wiser or steadier
when he comes within distance of it, or, as his
owner would say, when he "challenges" his leap,
and this enthusiast hardly overstates the truth

in affirming that his pupil "would change on the edge of a razor, and never let ye know he was off the Queen's high-road, God bless her, all the time!"

The Irishman, like the Arab, seems to possess a natural insight into the character of a horse; with many shortcomings as grooms, not the least of which are want of neatness in stable-management, and rooted dislike to hard work, except by fits and starts, they cherish extraordinary affection for their charges, and certainly in their dealings with them obviously prefer kindness to coercion. I do not think they always understand feeding judiciously, and many of them have much to learn about getting horses into condition; but they are unrivalled in teaching them to jump.

Though seldom practised, there is no better system in all undertakings than "to begin with the beginning," and an Irish horse-breaker is so persuaded of this great elementary truth that he never asks the colt to attempt three feet till it has become thoroughly master of two. With a cavesson rein, a handful of oats, and a few yards of waste ground behind the potato ground or the pig-styes, he will, by dint of skill and patience, turn the most blundering neophyte into an expert and stylish fencer in about six weeks. As he widens the ditch of his earthwork, he necessarily heightens its bank, which his simple tools, the spade and the pipe, soon raise to six or seven feet. When the young one has learned to surmount this temperately, but with courage, to change on the top, and deliver itself handsomely, with the requisite fling and freedom, on the far side, he considers it sufficiently advanced to take into the fields, where he leads it forthwith, leaving behind him the spade, but holding fast to the corn, the cavesson, and the pipe. Here he soon teaches his colt to wait, quietly grazing, or staring about, while he climbs the fence he intends it to jump, and almost before the long rein can be tightened it follows like a dog, to poke its nose in his hand for the few grains of oats it expects as a reward.

Some breakers drive their pupils from behind, with reins, pulling them up when they have accomplished the leap; but this is not so good a plan as necessitating the use of the whip, and having, moreover, a further disadvantage in accustoming the colt to stop dead short on landing, a habit productive hereafter of inconvenience to a loose rider taken unawares!

When he has taught his horse thus to *walk* over a country, for two or three miles on end, the breaker considers it, with reason, thoroughly trained for leaping, and has no hesitation, however low its condition, in riding it out with the hounds. Who that has hunted in Ireland but can recall the interest, and indeed amusement, with which he has watched some mere baby, strangely tackled and uncouthly equipped, sailing along in the front rank, steered with consummate skill and temper by a venerable rider who looks sixty on horseback, and at least eighty on foot. The man's dress is of the shabbiest and most incongruous, his boots are outrageous, his spurs ill put on, and his hat shows symptoms of ill-usage in warfare or the chase; but he sits in the saddle like a workman, and age has no more quenched the courage in his bright Irish eye, than it has soured the mirth of his temperament, or saddened the music of his brogue. You know instinctively that he must be a good fellow and a good sportsman; you cannot follow him for half a mile without being satisfied that he is a good rider, and you forget, in your admiration of his beast's performance, your surprise at its obvious youth, its excessive leanness, and the unusual shabbiness of its accoutrements. Inspecting these more narrowly, if you can get near enough, you begin to grudge the sums you have paid Bartley, or Wilkinson and Kidd, for the neat turn-out you have been taught to consider indispensable to success. You see that a horse may cross a dangerous country speedily and in safety, though its saddle be pulpy and weather-stained, with unequal stirrup-leathers, and only one girth;

though its bridle be a Pelham, *with* a noseband, and *without* a curb-chain, while one rein seems most untrustworthy, and the other, for want of a buckle, has its ends tied in a knot.   And yet, wherever the hounds go, thither follow this strangely-equipped pair.   They arrive at a seven-foot bank, defended by a wide and, more forbidding still, an enormously deep ditch on this side and with nothing apparently but blue sky on the other.   While the man utters an exclamation that seems a threat, a war-cry, and a shout of triumph combined, the horse springs to the summit, perches like a bird, and disappears buoyantly into space as if furnished, indeed, with wings, that it need only spread to fly away. They come to a stone-gap, as it is termed ; neither more nor less than a disused egress, made up with blocks of granite into a wall about five feet high, and the young one, getting close under it, clears the whole out of a trot, with the elasticity and the very action of a deer.   Presently some frightful chasm has to be encountered, wide enough for a brook, deep enough for a ravine, boggy of approach, faced with stone, and offering about as awkward an appearance as ever defeated a good man on his best hunter and bade him go to look for a better place.

Our friend in the bad hat, who knows what he is about, rides at this "yawner" a turn slower than would most Englishmen, and with a lighter hand on his horse's mouth, though his legs and knees are keeping the pupil well into its bridle, and, should the latter want to refuse, or "renage," as they say in Ireland, a disgrace of which it has not the remotest idea, there is a slip of ground-ash in the man's fingers ready to administer "a refresher" on its flank. "Did ye draw now?" asks an Irishman when his friend is describing how he accomplished some extraordinary feat in leaping, and the expression, derived from an obsolete custom of sticking the cutting - whip upright in the boot, so that it has come to mean punishment from that instrument, is nearly always answered—"I did *not*!" Light as a fairy, our young but experienced hunter dances down to the gulf, and leaves it behind with scarce an effort, while an unwashed hand bestows its caress on the reeking neck that will hereafter thicken prodigiously in some Saxon stable on a proper allowance of corn. If you are riding an Irish horse, you cannot do better than imitate closely every motion of the pair in front. If not, you will be wise, I think, to turn round and go home.

Presently we will hope, for the sake of the neophyte, whose condition is by no means on a par with his natural powers, the hounds either kill their fox, or run him to ground, or lose, or otherwise account for him, thus affording a few

minutes' repose for breathing or conversation.
"It's an intrickate country," observes some
brother-sportsman with just such another mount
to the veteran I have endeavoured to describe;
"and will that be the colt by Chitchat out of
Donovan's mare? Does he 'lep' well now?"
he adds, with much interest. "The beautifullest
ever ye see!" answers his friend, and nobody
who has witnessed the young horse's performances
can dispute the justice of such a reply. It is not
difficult to understand that hunters so educated
and so ridden in a country where every leap
requires power, courage, and the exercise of much
sagacity, should find little difficulty in surmount-
ing such obstacles as confront them on this side
of the Channel. It is child's play to fly a
Leicestershire fence, even with an additional rail,
for a horse that has been taught his business
amongst the precipitous banks and fathomless
ditches of Meath or Kildare. If the ground were
always sound and the hills somewhat levelled,
these Irish hunters would find little to stop them
in Leicestershire from going as straight as their
owners dared ride. Practice at walls renders
them clever timber-jumpers, they have usually
the spring and confidence that make nothing of a
brook, and their careful habit of preparing for
something treacherous on the landing side of
every leap prevents their being taken unawares

by the "oxers" and doubles that form such unwelcome exceptions to the usual run of impediments throughout the Shires. There is something in the expression of their very ears while we put them at their fences, that seems to say, "It's a good trick enough, and would take in most horses, but my mother taught me a thing or two in Connemara, and you don't come over me!" Unfortunately the Shires, as they are called *par excellence*, the Vale of Aylesbury, a perfect wilderness of grass, and indeed all the best hunting districts, ride very deep nine seasons out of ten, so that the Irish horse, accustomed to a sound limestone soil and an unfurrowed surface in his own green island, being moreover usually much wanting in condition, feels the added labour, and difference of action required, severely enough. It is proverbial that a horse equal to fourteen stone in Ireland is only up to thirteen in Leicestershire, and English purchasers must calculate accordingly.

But if some prize-taker at the Dublin Horse Show, or other ornament of that land which her natives call the "first flower of the earth and first gem of the sea," should disappoint you a little when you ride him in November from Ranksborough, the Coplow, Crick, Melton-Spinney, Christmas-Gorse, Great-Wood, or any other favourite covert in one of our many good hunting countries, do not therefore despond. If he fail in deep ground, or labour on ridge-and-furrow, remember he possesses this inestimable merit, that *he can go the shortest way!* Because the fence in front is large, black, and forbidding, you need not therefore send him at it a turn faster than usual ; he is accustomed to spring *from his back*, and cover large places out of a trot. If you ride your own line to hounds, it is no slight advantage thus to have the power of negotiating awkward corners, without being " committed to them " fifty yards off, unable to pull up should they prove impracticable ; and the faculty of "jumping at short notice," on this consideration alone, I conceive to be one of the choicest qualities a hunter can possess. Also, even in the most favoured and flying of the " grass countries," many fences require unusual steadiness and circumspection. If they are to be done at all, they can only be accomplished by creeping, some- times even *climbing* to the wished-for side. The front rank itself will probably shirk these un- accustomed obstacles with cordial unanimity, leaving them to be triumphantly disposed of by your new purchase from Kildare. He pokes out his nose, as if to inspect the depth of a possible interment, and it is wise to let him manage it all his own way. You give him his head, and the slightest possible kick in the ribs. With a cringe of his powerful back and quarters, a vigorous lift that seems to reach two-thirds of the required distance, a second spring, apparently taken from a twig weak enough to bend under a bird, that covers the remainder, a scramble for foothold, a half-stride, and a snort of satisfaction, the whole is disposed of, and you are alone with the hounds.

Though, under such circumstances, these seem pretty sure to run to ground or otherwise disappoint you within half a mile, none the less credit is due to your horse's capabilities, and you vow next season to have nothing but Irish nags in your stable, resolving for the future to ride straighter than you have ever done before.

But if you are so well pleased now with your promising Patlander, what shall you think of him this time next year, when he has had twelve months of your stud-groom's stable-management, and consumed ten or a dozen quarters of good English oats? Though you may have bought him as a six-year-old, he will have grown in size and substance, even in height, and will not only look, but feel up to a stone more weight than you ever gave him credit for. He can jump when he is blown *now*, but he will never be blown *then*. Condition will teach him to laugh at the deep ground, while his fine shoulders and true shape will enable him, after the necessary practice, to travel across ridge-and-furrow without a lurch.

IRISH HUNTERS

He will have turned out a rattling good horse, and you will never grudge the cheque you wrote, nor the punch you were obliged to drink, before his late proprietor would let you make him your own.

Gold and whisky, in large quantities and judiciously applied, may no doubt buy the best horses in Ireland. But a man must know where to look for them, and even in remote districts will sometimes be disappointed to find that the English dealers have forestalled him. Happily, there are so many good horses, perhaps I should say so few *rank bad ones*, bred in the country, that from the very sweepings and leavings of the market, one need not despair of turning up a trump. A hunter is in so far like a wife, that experience alone will prove whether he is or is not good for nothing. Make and shape, in either case, may be perfect, pedigree unimpeachable, and manners blameless, but who is to answer for temper, reflection, docility, and the generous staying power that accepts rough and smooth, ups and downs, good and evil, without a struggle or a sob? When we have tried them, we find them out, and can only make the best of our disappointment, if they do not fully come up to our expectations.

There is many a good hunter, particularly in a rich man's stable, that never has a chance of proving its value. With three or four, we know their form to a pound; with a dozen, season after season goes by without furnishing occasion for the use of all, till some fine scenting day, after mounting a friend, we are surprised to learn that the flower of the whole stud has hitherto been esteemed but a moderate animal, only fit to carry the sandwiches, and bring us home.

I imagine, notwithstanding all we have heard and read concerning the difficulty of buying Irish horses in their own country, that there are still scores of them in Cork, Limerick, and other breeding districts, as yet unpromised and unsold. The scarcity of weight-carriers is indisputable, but can we find them here? The "light man's horse," to fly under sixteen stone, is a "black swan" everywhere, and if *not* "a light man's horse," that is to say, free, flippant, fast, and well-bred, he will never give his stalwart rider thorough satisfaction; but in Ireland, far more plentifully than in England, are still to be found handsome, clever, hunting-like animals fit to carry thirteen stone, and capital jumpers at reasonable prices, varying from one to two hundred pounds. The latter sum, particularly if you had it with you in *sovereigns*, would in most localities ensure the "pick of the basket," and ten or twenty of the coins thrown back for luck.

I have heard it objected to Irish hunters, that

"This strangely equipped pair"

they are so accustomed to "double" all their
places, as to practise this accomplishment even at
those flying fences of the grazing districts which
ought to be taken in the stride, and that they
require fresh tuition before they can be trusted at
the staked-and-bound or the bullfinch, lest, catching their feet in the growers as in a net, they
should be tumbled headlong to the ground. I
can only say that I have been well and safely
carried by many of them on their first appearance
in Leicestershire, as in other English countries,
that they seemed intuitively to apprehend the
character of the fences they had to deal with, and
that, although being mortal, they could not always
keep on their legs, I cannot remember one of
them giving me a fall *because* he was an Irish
horse!

How many their nationality has saved me, I
forbear to count, but I am persuaded that the
careful tuition undergone in youth, and their
varied experience when sufficiently advanced to
follow hounds over their native country, imparts
that facility of powerful and safe jumping, which
is one of the most important qualities among the
many that constitute a hunter.

They possess also the merit of being universally
well-bred. This is an advantage no sportsman
will overlook who likes to be near hounds while
they run, but objects to leading, driving, or

perhaps *pushing* his horse home. Till within a few years, there was literally *no* cart-horse blood in Ireland. The "black-drop" of the ponderous Clydesdale remained positively unknown, and although the Suffolk Punch has been recently introduced, he cannot yet have sufficiently tainted the pedigrees of the country, to render us mistrustful of a golden-coated chestnut, with a round barrel and a strong back.

No, their horses, if not quite "clean-bred," as the Irish themselves call it, are at least of illustrious parentage on both sides a few generations back, and this high descent cannot but avail them when called on for long-continued exertion, particularly at the end of the day.

Juvenal, hurling his scathing satire against the patricians of his time, drew from the equine race a metaphor to illustrate the superiority of merit over birth. However unanswerable in argument, he was, I think, wrong in his facts. Men and women are to be found of every parentage, good, bad, and indifferent; but with horses, there is more in race than in culture, and for the selection of these noble animals at least, I can imagine no safer guide than the aristocratic maxim, "Blood will tell!"

CHAPTER X

THOROUGH-BRED HORSES

I HAVE heard it affirmed, though I know not on what authority, that if we are to believe the hunting records of the last hundred years, in all runs so severe and protracted as to admit of only one man getting to the finish, this exceptional person was, in *every* instance, riding an old horse, a thorough-bred horse, and a horse under fifteen-two!

Perhaps on consideration, this is a less remarkable statement than it appears. That the survivor was an old horse, means that he had many years of corn and condition to pull him through; that he was a little horse, infers he carried a light weight, but that he was a thorough-bred horse seems to me a reasonable explanation of the whole.

"The thorough-bred ones never stop," is a common saying among sportsmen, and there are daily instances of some high-born steed who can boast

"His sire from the desert, his dam from the north,"

galloping steadily on, calm and vigorous, when the country behind him is dotted for miles with hunters standing still in every field.

It is obvious that a breed, reared expressly for racing purposes, must be the fastest of its kind. A colt considered good enough to be "put through the mill" on Newmarket Heath, or Middleham Moor, whatever may be his short-comings in the select company he finds at school, cannot but seem "a flyer," when in after-life he meets horses, however good, that have neither been bred nor trained for the purpose of galloping a single mile at the rate of an express train. While these are at speed he is only cantering, and we need not therefore be surprised that he can keep cantering on after they are reduced to a walk.

In the hunting-field, "what kills is the pace." When hounds can make it good enough they kill their fox, when horses *cannot* it kills *them*, and for this reason alone, if for no other, I would always prefer that my hunters should be quite thorough-bred.

Though undoubtedly the best, I cannot affirm, however, that they are always the *pleasantest* mounts; far from it, indeed, just at first, though subsequent superiority makes amends for the little eccentricities of gait and temper peculiar to pupils from the racing-stable in their early youth.

THOROUGH-BRED HORSES

An idle, lurching mover, rather narrow before the saddle, with great power of back and loins, a habit of bearing on its rider's hand, one side to its mouth, and a loose neck, hardly inspires a careful man with the confidence necessary for enjoyment ; coming away from Ranksborough, for instance, downhill, with the first fence leaning towards him, very little room, his horse too much extended, going on its shoulders, and getting the better of him at every stride !

But this is an extreme case, purposely chosen to illustrate at their worst the disadvantages of riding a thorough-bred horse.

It is often our own fault, when we buy one of these illustrious cast-offs, that our purchase so disappoints us after we have got it home. Many men believe that to carry them through an exhausting run, such staying powers are required as win under high weights and at long distances on the turf.

Their selection, therefore, from the racing-stable is some young one of undeniably stout blood, that when "asked the question" for the first time, has been found too slow to put in training. They argue with considerable show of reason, that it will prove quite speedy enough for a hunter, but they forget that though a fast horse is by no means indispensable to the chase, a *quick* one is most conducive to enjoyment when we are compelled to jump all sorts of fences out of all sorts of ground.

Now a yearling, quick enough on its legs to promise a turn of speed, is pretty sure to be esteemed worth training, nor will it be condemned as useless till its distance is found to be just short of half a mile. In plain English, when it fails under the strain on wind and frame, of galloping at its very best, eight hundred and seventy yards, and "fades to nothing" in the next ten.

Now this collapse is really more a question of speed than stamina. There is a want of reach or leverage somewhere, that makes its rapid action too laborious to be lasting, but there is no reason why the animal that comes short of five furlongs on the trial-ground, should not hold its own in front, for five miles of a steeplechase, or fifteen of a run with hounds.

These, in fact, are the so-called "weeds" that win our cross-country races, and when we reflect on the pace and distance of the Liverpool, four miles and three-quarters run in something under eleven minutes, at anything but feather-weights, and over all sorts of fences, we cannot but admire the speed, gallantry, and endurance, the essentially *game* qualities of our English horse. And here I may observe that a good steeplechaser, properly sobered and brought into his bridle, is one of the pleasantest hunters a man can ride, particularly in a flying country. He is sure to be able to "make haste" in all sorts of ground, while the smooth, easy stride that wins between the flags is invaluable through dirt. He does not lose his head and turn foolish, as do many good useful hunters, when bustled along for a mile or two at something like racing pace. Very quick over his fences, his style of jumping is no less conducive to safety than despatch, while his courage is sure to be undeniable, because the slightest tendency to refuse would have disqualified him for success in his late profession, wherein, also, he must necessarily have learnt to be a free and brilliant water-jumper.

Indeed, you may always take *two* liberties with a steeplechase horse during a run (not more). The first time you squeeze him, he thinks, "Oh! this is the brook!" and putting on plenty of steam, flings himself as far as ever he can. The second, he accepts your warning with equal goodwill. "All right!" he seems to answer; "this is the brook, coming home!" But if you try the same game a third time, I cannot undertake to say what may happen; you will probably puzzle him exceedingly, upset his temper, and throw him out of gear for the day.

We have travelled a long way, however, from our original subject, tuition of the thorough-bred for the field, or perhaps I should call it the task of turning a bad race-horse into a good hunter.

Like every other process of education, this requires exceeding perseverance, and a patience not to be overcome. The irritation of a moment may undo the lessons of a week, and if the master forgets himself, you may be sure the pupil will long remember which of the two was in fault. Never begin a quarrel if it can possibly be avoided, because, when war is actually declared, you must fight it out to the bitter end, and if you are beaten, you had better send your horse to Tattersall's, for you will never be master again.

Stick to him till he does what you require, trusting, nevertheless, rather to time than violence, and if you can get him at last to obey you of his own free will, without knowing why, I cannot repeat too often, you will have won the most conclusive of victories.

When the late Sir Charles Knightley took Sir Marinel out of training, and brought him down to Pytchley, to teach him the way he should go (and the way of Sir Charles over a country was that of a bird in the air), he found the horse restive, ignorant, wilful, and unusually averse to learning the business of a hunter. The animal was, however, well worth a little painstaking, and his owner, a perfect Centaur in the saddle, rode him out for a lesson in jumping

the first day the hounds remained in the kennel.
At two o'clock, as his old friend and contemporary,
Mr. John Cooke, informed me, he came back,
having failed to get the rebel over a single fence.
"But I have told them not to take his saddle off,"
said Sir Charles, sitting down to a cutlet and a
glass of Madeira ; "after luncheon I mean to have
a turn at him again !"

So the baronet remounted and took the lesson
up where he had left off. Nerve, temper,
patience, the strongest seat, and the finest hands
in England, could not but triumph at last, and
this thorough-bred pair came home at dinner-
time, having larked over all the stiffest fences in
the country, with perfect unanimity and goodwill. Sir Marinel, and Benvolio, also a thorough-
bred horse, were by many degrees, Sir Charles
has often told me, the best hunters he ever had.

Shuttlecock, too, immortalised in the famous
Billesdon Coplow poem, when

> "Villiers esteemed it a serious bore,
>   That no longer could Shuttlecock fly as before,"

was a clean thorough-bred horse, fast enough to
have made a good figure on the racecourse, but
with a rooted disinclination to jump.

That king of horsemen, the grandfather of
the present Lord Jersey, whom I am proud to
remember having seen ride fairly away from a
whole Leicestershire field, over a rough country

not far from Melton, at seventy-three, told me
that his horse, though it turned out eventually
one of his safest and boldest fencers, at the end
of six weeks' tuition would not jump the leaping-
bar the height of its own knees! His lordship,
however, who was blessed in perfection with the
sweet temper, as with the personal beauty and
gallant bearing of his race, neither hurried nor
ill-used it, and the time spent on the animal's
education, though somewhat wearisome, was not
thrown away.

Mr. Gilmour's famous *Vingt-et-un*, the best
hunter, he protests, by a great deal that gentleman ever possessed, was quite thorough-bred.
Seventeen hands high, but formed all over in
perfect proportion to this commanding frame, it
may easily be imagined that the power and stride
of so large an animal made light of ordinary
obstacles; and I do not believe, though it may
sound an extravagant assertion, there was a fence
in the whole of Leicestershire that could have
stopped *Vingt-et-un* and his rider, on a good
scenting day some few years ago. Such men
and such horses ought never to grow old.

Mr. William Cooke, too, owned a celebrated
hunter called Advance, of stainless pedigree, as
was December, so named from being foaled on
the last day of that month, a premature arrival
that lost him his year for racing purposes by

twenty-four hours, and transferred the colt to the hunting-stables. Mr. Cooke rode nothing but this class, nor indeed could any animal less speedy than a race-horse, sustain the pace he liked to go.

Whitenose, a beautiful animal that the late Sir Richard Sutton affirmed was not only the best hunter he ever owned, but that he ever saw or heard of, and on whose back he is painted in Sir F. Grant's spirited picture of the Cottesmore Meet, was also quite thorough-bred. When Sir Richard hunted the Burton country, Whitenose carried him through a run so severe in pace and of such long duration, that not another horse got to the end, galloping, his master assured me, steadily on without a falter, to the last. By the way, he was then of no great age, and nearer sixteen hands than fifteen-two! This was a very easy horse to ride, and could literally jump anything he got his nose over. A picture to look at, with a coat like satin, the eyes of a deer, and the truest action in his slow as in his fast paces, he has always been my ideal of perfection in a hunter.

But it would be endless to enumerate the many examples I can recall of the thorough-bred's superiority in the hunting-field. Those I have mentioned belong to a bygone time, but a man need not look very narrowly into any knot of sportsmen at the present day, particularly *after* a sharpish scurry in deep ground, before his eye rests on the thin tail, and smoothly turned quarters, that need no gaudier blazon to attest the nobility of their descent.

If you mean, however, to ride a thorough-bred one, and choose to *make* him yourself, do not feel disappointed that he seems to require more time and tuition than his lower-born cousins, once and twice removed.

In the first place you will begin by thinking him wanting in courage! Where the half-bred one, eager, flurried, and excited, rushes wildly at an unaccustomed difficulty, your calmer gentleman proceeds deliberately to examine its nature, and consider how he can best accomplish his task. It is not that he has less valour, but more discretion! In the monotonous process of training, he has acquired, with other tiresome tricks, the habit of doing as little as he can, in the different paces, walk, canter, and gallop, of which he has become so weary. Even the excitement of hunting till hounds *really* run, hardly dissipates his aristocratic lethargy, but only get him in front for one of those scurries that, perhaps twice in a season, turn up a fox in twenty minutes, and if you *dare* trust him, you will be surprised at the brilliant performance of your idle, negligent, wayward young friend.

THOROUGH-BRED HORSES

He bends kindly to the bridle he objected to all the morning, he tucks his quarters in, and *scours* through the deep ground like a hare, he slides over råther than jumps his fences, with the easy swoop of a bird on the wing, and when everything of meaner race has been disposed of a field or two behind, he trots up to some high bit of timber, and leaps it gallantly without a pause, though only yesterday he would have turned round to kick at it for an hour!

Still, there are many chances against your having such an opportunity as this. Most days the hounds do *not* run hard. When they do, you are perhaps so unfortunate as to lose your start, and finally, should everything else be in your favour, it is twenty to one you are riding the wrong horse!

Therefore, the process of educating your young one must be conducted on quieter principles, and in a less haphazard way. If you can find a pack of harriers, and *their master does not object*, there is no better school for the troublesome or unwilling pupil. But remember, I entreat, that horsebreaking is prejudicial to sport, and most unwelcome. You are there on sufferance, take care to interfere with nobody, and above all, keep wide of the hounds! The great advantage you will find in hare-hunting over the wilder pursuit of the fox, is in the circles described by your game. There is plenty of time to "have it out" with a refuser, and indeed to turn him backwards and forwards if you please, over the same leap, without fear of being left behind. The "merry harriers" are pretty sure to return in a few minutes, and you can begin again, with as much enthusiasm of man and horse as if you had never been out of the hunt at all! Whip and spur, I need hardly insist, cannot be used too sparingly, and anything in the shape of haste or over-anxiety is prejudicial, but if it induces him to jump in his stride, you may ride this kind of horse a turn faster at his fences than any other. You can trust him not to be in too great a hurry, and it is his nature to take care of himself. Till he has become thoroughly accustomed to his new profession, it is well to avoid such places as seem particularly distasteful and likely to make him rebel. His fine skin will cause him to be a little shy of thick bullfinches, and his sagacity mistrusts deep or blind ditches, such as less intelligent animals would run into without a thought. Rather select rails, or clean upright fences, that he can compass and understand. Try to imbue him with love for the sport and confidence in his rider. After a few weeks, he will turn his head from nothing, and go straighter, as well as faster, and longer than anything in your stable.

An old Meltonian used to affirm that the first

two articles of his creed for the hunting season
were, "a perfectly pure claret, and thorough-bred
horses." Of the former he was unsparing to his
friends, the latter he used freely enough for
himself. Certainly no man gave pleasanter
dinners, or was better carried, and one might do
worse than go to Melton with implicit reliance
on these twin accessories of the chase. All
opinions must be agreed, I fancy, about the one,
but there are still many prejudices against the
other. Heavy men especially declare they cannot
find thorough-bred horses to carry them, for-
getting, it would seem, that size is no more a
criterion of strength than haste is of speed. The
bone of a thorough-bred horse is of the closest
and toughest fibre, his muscles are well-developed,
and his joints elastic. Do not these advantages
infer power, no less than stamina, and in our own
experience have we not all reason to corroborate
the old-fashioned maxim, "It is action that
carries weight"? Nimrod, who understood the
subject thoroughly, observes with great truth,
that "'Wind' is strength ; when a horse is
blown, a mountain or a molehill are much the
same to him," and no sportsman who has ever
scaled a Highland hill to circumvent a red deer,
or walk up to "a point," will dispute the
argument. What a game animal it is, that
without touch of spur, at the mere pleasure and

caprice of a rider, struggles gallantly on till it drops!

There used to be a saying in the prize ring, that "Seven pounds will lick the best man in England." This is but a technical mode of stating that, *cæteris paribus*, weight means strength. Thirty years ago, it was a common practice at Melton to weigh hunters after they were put in condition, and sportsmen often wondered to find how the eye had deceived them, in the comparative tonnage, so to speak, and consequently the horse-power of these different conveyances; the thorough-bred, without exception, proving far heavier than was supposed.

An athlete, we all know, whether boxer, wrestler, pedestrian, cricketer, or gymnast, looks smaller in his clothes, and larger when he is stripped. Similarly, on examining in the stable, "the nice little horse" we admired in the field, it surprises us to find nearly sixteen hands of height, and six feet of girth, with power to correspond, in an animal of which we thought the only defect was want of size. A thorough-bred one is invariably a little bigger and a great deal stronger than he looks. Of his power to carry weight, those tall, fine men who usually ride so judiciously and so straight, are not yet sufficiently convinced, although if you ask any celebrated "welter" to name the best horse he ever had, he is sure to answer, "Oh! little So-and-so. He wasn't up to my weight, but he carried me better than anything else in the stable!" Surely no criterion could be more satisfactory than this!

It may not be out of place to observe here, as an illustration of the well-known maxim, "Horses can go in all shapes," that of the three heaviest men I can call to mind who rode perfectly straight to hounds, the best hunter owned by each was too long in the back. "Sober Robin," an extraordinary animal that could carry Mr. Richard Gurney, riding twenty stone, ahead of all the light-weights, was thus shaped. A famous bay-horse, nearly as good, belonging to the late Mr. Wood of Brixworth Hall, an equally heavy man, who when thus mounted never stopped to open a gate! had, his owner used to declare, as many vertebræ as a crocodile; and Colonel Wyndham, whose size and superiority in the saddle I have already mentioned, hesitated a week before he bought his famous black mare, the most brilliant hunter he ever possessed, because she was at least three inches too long behind the saddle!

I remember also seeing the late Lord Mayo ride fairly away from a Pytchley field, no easy task, between Lilbourne and Cold Ashby, on a horse that except for its enormous depth of girth, arguing unfailing wind, seemed to have no good points whatever to catch the eye. It was tall, narrow, plain-headed, with very bad shoulders, and very long legs, all this to carry at least eighteen stone ; but it was nearly, if not quite, thorough-bred.

We need hardly dwell on the advantages of speed and endurance, inherited from the Arab, and improved, as we fondly hope, almost to perfection, through the culture of many generations, while even the fine temper of the "desert-born" has not been so warped by the tricks of stable-boys, and the severity of turf-discipline, but that a little forbearance and kind usage soon restores its natural docility.

In all the qualities of a hunter, the thorough-bred horse is, I think, superior to the rest of his kind. You can hardly do better than buy one, and "make him to your hand," should you be blessed with good nerves, a fine temper, and a delicate touch, or, wanting these qualities, confide him to someone so gifted, if you wish to be carried well and pleasantly, in your love for hunting, perhaps I should rather say, for the keen and stirring excitement we call "riding to hounds."

CHAPTER XI

RIDING TO FOX-HOUNDS

" IF you want to be near hounds," says an old friend of mine who, for a lifetime, has religiously practised what he preaches, "the method is simple, and seems only common-sense —*keep as close to them as ever you can !*" but I think, though, with his undaunted nerve, and extraordinary horsemanship, he seems to find it feasible enough, this plan, for most people, requires considerable management, and no little modification.

I grant we should never let them slip away from us, and that, in nine cases out of ten, when defeated by what we choose to call "a bad turn" it is our own fault. At the same time there are many occasions on which a man who keeps his eyes open, and knows how to ride, can save his horse to some purpose, by travelling inside the pack, and galloping a hundred yards for their three.

I say *who keeps his eyes open*, because, in order

to effect this economy of speed and distance, it is indispensable to watch their doings narrowly, and to possess the experience that tells one when they are *really* on the line, and when only flinging forward to regain, with the dash that is a foxhound's chief characteristic, the scent they have overrun. Constant observation will alone teach us to distinguish the hounds that are right ; and to turn with them judiciously is the great secret of "getting to the end."

We must, therefore, be within convenient distance, and to ensure such proximity it is most desirable to get a good start. Let us begin at the beginning, and consider how this primary essential is to be obtained.

Directly a move is made from the place of meeting, it is well to cut short all "coffee-house" conversation, even at the risk of neglecting certain social amenities, and to fix our minds at once on the work in hand. A good story, though pleasant enough in its way, cannot compare with a good run, and it is quite possible to lose the one by too earnest attention to the other.

A few courteous words previously addressed to the huntsman will ensure his civility during the day ; but this is not a happy moment for imparting to him your opinion on things in general and his own business in particular. He has many matters to occupy his thoughts, and does not care

to see you in the middle of his favourites on a
strange horse. It is better to keep the second
whip between yourself and the hounds, jogging
calmly on, with a pleasant view of their well-
filled backs and handsomely-carried sterns, taking
care to pull up, religiously murmuring the orthodox
caution—"Ware horse!" when any one of them
requires to pause for any purpose. You cannot
too early impress on the hunt servants that you
are a lover of the animal, most averse to interfering with it at all times, and especially in the
ardour of the chase. If the size and nature of the
covert will admit, you had better go into it with
the hounds, and on this occasion, but no other, I
think it is permissible to make use of the huntsman's pilotage at a respectful distance. Where
there are foxes there is game, where game, riot.
A few young hounds must come out with every
pack, and the *rate* or *cheer* of your leader will
warn you whether their opening music means a
false flourish or a welcome find. Also where he
goes you can safely follow, and need have no
misgivings that the friendly hand-gate for which
he is winding down some tortuous ride will be
nailed up.

Besides, though floundering in deep, sloughy
woodlands entails considerable labour on your
horse, it is less distressing than that gallop of a
mile or two at speed which endeavours, but

usually fails, to make amends for a bad start ;
whereas, if you get away on good terms, you can
indulge him with a pull at the first opportunity,
and those scenting days are indeed rare on which
hounds run many fields without at least a hover,
if not a check.

Some men take their station outside the
covert, down wind, in a commanding position,
so as to hear every turn of the hounds,
secure a front place for the sport, and—head
the fox !

But we will suppose all such difficulties overcome ; that a little care, attention, and common-
sense have enabled you to get away on good
terms with the pack ; and that you emerge not a
bowshot off, while they stream across the first field
with a dash that brings the mettle to your heart
and the blood to your brain. Do not, therefore,
lose your head. It is the characteristic of good
manhood to be physically calm in proportion to
moral excitement. Remember there are two
occasions in chase when the manner of hounds is
not to be trusted. On first coming away with
their fox, and immediately before they kill him,
the steadiest will lead you to believe there is a
burning scent and that they cannot make a
mistake. Nevertheless, hope for the best, set
your horse going, and if, as you sail over, or
crash through, the first fence, you mark the pack

driving eagerly on, drawn to a line at either end by the pace, harden your heart, and thank your stars. It is all right, you may lay odds, you are in for a really good thing!

I suppose I need hardly observe that the laws of fox-hunting forbid you to follow hounds by the very obvious process of galloping in their track. Nothing makes them so wild, to use the proper term, as "riding on their line"; and should you be ignorant enough to attempt it, you are pretty sure to be told *where* you are driving them, and desired to go there yourself!

No; you must keep one side or the other, but do not, if you can help it, let the nature of the obstacles to be encountered bias your choice. Ride for ground as far as possible when the foothold is good; the fences will take care of themselves; but let no advantages of sound turf, nor even open gates, tempt you to stray more than a couple of hundred yards from the pack. At that distance a bad turn can be remedied, and a good one gives you leisure to pull back into a trot. Remember, too, that it is the nature of a fox, and we are now speaking of fox-hunting, to travel down wind; therefore, as a general rule, keep to leeward of the hounds. Every bend they make ought to be in your favour; but, on the other hand, should they chance to turn up wind, they will begin to run very hard, and this is a good reason for never letting them get, so to speak, out of your reach. I repeat, as a *general rule*, but by no means without exception. In Leicestershire especially, foxes seem to scorn this fine old principle, and will make their point with a stiff breeze blowing in their teeth; but on such occasions they do not usually mean to go very far, and the gallant veteran, with his white tag, that gives you the run to be talked of for years, is almost always a wind-sinker from wold or woodland in an adjoining hunt.

Suppose, however, the day is perfectly calm, and there seems no sufficient reason to prefer one course to the other, should we go to right or left? This is a matter in which neither precept nor personal experience can avail. One man is as sure to do right as the other to do wrong. There is an intuitive perception, more animal than human, of what we may call "the line of chase," with which certain sportsmen are gifted by nature, and which, I believe, would bring them up at critical points of the finest and longest runs if they came out hunting in a gig. This faculty, where everything else is equal, causes A to ride better than B, but is no less difficult to explain than the instinct that guides an Indian on the prairie or a swallow across the sea. It counsels the lady in her carriage, or the old coachman piloting her children on their ponies, it enables the butcher to come up on his hack, the first-flight man to save his horse, and above all, the huntsman to kill his fox.

The Duke of Beaufort possesses it in an extra-ordinary degree. When so crippled by gout, or reduced by suffering as to be unable to keep the saddle over a fence, he seems, even in strange countries, to see no less of the sport than in old days, when he could ride into every field with his hounds. And I do believe that now, in any part of Gloucestershire, with ten couple of "the badger-pyed" and a horn, he could go out and kill his fox in a Bath-chair!

Perhaps, however, his may be an extreme case. No man has more experience, few such a natural aptitude and fondness for the sport. Lord Worcester, too, like his father, has shown how an educated gentleman, with abilities equal to all exigencies of a high position that affords com-paratively little leisure for the mere amusements of life, can excel, in their own profession, men who have been brought up to it from childhood, whose thoughts and energies, winter and summer, morning, noon, and night, are concentrated on the business of the chase.

This knack of getting to hounds, then—should we consider genius or talent too strong terms to use for proficiency in field sports—while a most valuable quality to everybody who comes out hunting, is no less rare than precious. If we have it, we are to be congratulated and our horses still more, but if, like the generality of men, we have it *not*, let us consider how far common-sense and close attention will supply the want of a natural gift.

It was said of an old friend of mine, the keenest of the keen, that he always rode as if he had never seen a run before, and should never see a run again! This, I believe, is something of the feeling with which we ought to be possessed, impelling us to take every legitimate advantage and to throw no possible chance away. It cannot be too often repeated that judicious choice of ground is the very first essential for success. Therefore the hunting - field has always been considered so good a school for cavalry officers. There seems no limit to the endurance of a horse in travelling over a hard and tolerably level surface, even under heavy weight, but we all know the fatal effect of a very few yards in a steam - ploughed field, when the gallant animal sinks to its hocks every stride. Keep an eye forward, then, and shape your course where the foothold is smooth and sound. In a hilly country choose the sides of the slopes, above, rather than below, the pack, for if they turn away from you, it is harder work to gallop up than down. In

the latter case, and for this little hint I am
indebted to Lord Wilton, do not increase your
speed so as to gain in distance, rather preserve
the same regular pace, so as to save in wind.
Descending an incline at an easy canter, and held
well together, your horse is resting almost as if
he were standing still. It is quite time enough
when near the bottom to put on a spurt that will
shoot him up the opposite rise.

On the grass, if you *must* cross ridge-and-
furrow, take it a-slant, your horse will pitch less
on his shoulders, and move with greater ease,
while if they lie the right way, by keeping him
on the crest, rather than in the trough of those
long parallel rollers, you will ensure firm ground
for his gallop, and a sounder, as well as higher
take-off for the leap, when he comes to his
fence.

I need hardly remind you that in all swampy
places, rushes may be trusted implicitly, and
experienced hunters seem as well aware of the
fact as their riders. Vegetable growth, indeed,
of any kind has a tendency to suck moisture into
its fibres, and consequently to drain, more or less,
the surface in its immediate vicinity. The deep
rides of a woodland are least treacherous at their
edges, and the brink of a brook is most reliable
close to some pollard or alder bush, particularly
on the upper side, as Mr. Bromley Davenport

knew better than most people, when he wrote his thrilling lines :—

> "Then steady, my young one! the place I've selected
> Above the dwarf willow, is sound, I'll be bail;
> With your muscular quarters beneath you collected,
> Prepare for a rush like the limited mail!"

But we cannot always be on the grass, nor, happily, are any of us obliged, often in a lifetime, to ride at the Whissendine!

In ploughed land, choose a wet furrow, for the simple reason that water would not stand in it unless the bottom were hard, but if you cannot find one, nor a footpath, nor a cart-track trampled down into a certain consistency, remember the fable of the hare and the tortoise, pull your horse back into a trot, and never fear but that you will be able to make up your leeway when you arrive at better ground. It is fortunate that the fences are usually less formidable here than in the pastures, and will admit of creeping into, and otherwise negotiating, with less expenditure of power, so you may travel pretty safely, and turn at pleasure, shorter than the hounds.

There *are* plough countries, notably in Gloucestershire and Wilts, that ride light. To them the above remarks in no way apply. Enclosed with stone walls, if there is anything like a scent, hounds carry such a head, and run so hard over these districts, that you must simply go as fast as your horse's pace, and as straight as his courage admits, but if you have the Duke of Beaufort's dog-pack in front of you, do not be surprised to find, with their extraordinary dash and enormous stride, that even on the pick of your stable, ere you can jump into one field they are half-way across the next.

In hunting, as in everything else, compensation seems the rule of daily life, and the very brilliancy of the pace affords its own cure. Either hounds run into their fox, or, should he find room to turn, flash over the scent, and bring themselves to a check. You will not then regret having made play while you could, and although no good sportsman, and, indeed, no kind-hearted man, would overtax the powers of the most generous animal in creation, still we must remember that we came out for the purpose of seeing the fun, and unless we can keep near the hounds while they run we shall lose many beautiful instances of their sagacity when brought to their noses, and obliged to hunt.

There is no greater treat to a lover of the chase than to watch a pack of high-bred fox-hounds that have been running hard on pasture, brought suddenly to a check on the dusty sun-dried fallows. After dashing and snatching in vain for a furlong or so, they will literally quarter their ground like pointers, till they recover the line, every yard of which they make good, with noses down and sterns working as if from the concentrated energy of all their faculties, till suspicion becomes certainty, and they lay themselves out once more, in the uncontrolled ecstasy of pursuit.

Now if you are a mile behind, you miss all these interesting incidents, and lose, as does your disappointed hunter, more than half the amusement you both came out to enjoy. The latter, too, works twice as hard when held back in the rear, as when ridden freely and fearlessly in front. The energy expended in fighting with his rider would itself suffice to gallop many a furlong and leap many a fence, while the moral effect of disappointment is most disheartening to a creature of such a highly-strung nervous organisation. Look at the work done by a huntsman's horse before the very commencement of some fine run, the triumphant conclusion of which depends so much on his freshness at the finish, and yet how rarely does he succumb to the labour of love imposed ; but then he usually leaves the covert in close proximity to his friends the hounds, every minute of his toil is cheered by their companionship, and, having no leeway to make up he need not be overpaced when they are running their hardest, while he finds a moment's leisure to recover himself when they are hunting their closest and best. In those

long and severe chases, to which, unhappily, two
or three horses may sometimes be sacrificed, the
"first flight" are not usually sufferers. Death
from exhaustion is more likely to be inflicted
cruelly, though unwittingly, on his faithful friend
and comrade, by the injudicious and hesitating
rider, who has neither decision to seize a commanding position in front, nor self-denial to be
satisfied with an unassuming retirement in rear.
His valour and discretion are improperly mixed,
like bad punch, and fatal is the result. A timely
pull means simply the difference between breathlessness and exhaustion, but this opportune relief
is only available for him who knows exactly how
far they brought it, and where the hounds flashed
beyond the line of their fox at a check.

I remember in my youth, alas! long ago, "the
old sportsman"—a character for whom, I fear,
we entertained in my day less veneration than we
professed—amongst many inestimable precepts
was fond of propounding the following :—

"Young gentleman, nurse your hunter carefully
at the beginning of a run, and when the others
are tired he will enable you to see the end."

Now, with all due deference to the old sportsman, I take leave to differ with him *in toto*. By
nursing one's horse, I conclude he meant riding
him at less than half-speed during that critical
ten minutes when hounds run their very hardest

and straightest.   If we follow this cautious advice, who is to solve the important question, "Which way are they gone?" when we canter anxiously up to a sign-post where four roads meet, with a fresh and eager horse indeed, but not the wildest notion towards which point of the compass we should direct his energies?   We can but stop to listen, take counsel of a countryman who un-wittingly puts us wrong, ride to points, speculate on chances, and make up our minds never to be really on terms with them again!

No, I think on the contrary, the best and most experienced riders adopt a very different system. On the earliest intimation that hounds are "away," they may be observed getting after them with all the speed they can make.   Who ever saw Mr. Portman, for instance, trotting across the first field when his bitches were well out of covert settling on the line of their fox?—and I only mention his name because it occurs to me at the moment, and because, notwithstanding the formidable hills of his wild country and the pace of his flying pack, he is always present at the finish, to render them assistance if required, as it often must be, with a sinking fox.

"The first blow is half the battle" in many nobler struggles than a street brawl with a cad, and the very speed at which you send your horse along for a few furlongs, if the ground is at all favourable, enables you to give him a pull at the earliest opportunity, without fear lest the whole distant panorama of the hunt should fade into space while you are considering what to do next.

Not that I mean you to over-mark, or push him for a single stride, beyond the collected pace at which he travels with ease and comfort to himself ; for remember he is as much your partner as the fairest young lady ever trusted to your guidance in a ballroom : but I *do* mean that you should make as much haste as is compatible with your mutual enjoyment, and, reflecting on the capricious nature of scent, take the chance of its failure, to afford you a moment's breathing-time when most required.

At all periods of a fox-chase, be careful to *anticipate a check.* Never with more foresight than when flying along in the ecstasy of a quick thing, on a brilliant hunter. Keep an eye forward, and scan with close attention every moving object in front. There you observe a flock of sheep getting into line like cavalry for a charge—that is where the fox has gone. Or perhaps a man is ploughing half a mile farther on ; in all probability this object will have headed him, and on the discretion with which you ride at these critical moments may depend the per-formance of the pack, the difference between "a beautiful turn" and "an unlucky check." The very rush of your gallop alongside them will tempt high-mettled hounds into the indiscretion of overrunning their scent. Whereas, if you take a pull at your horse, and give them plenty of room, they will swing to the line, and wheel like a flock of pigeons on the wing.

Always ride, then, to *command* hounds if you can, but never be tempted, when in this proud position, to press them, and to spoil your own sport, with that of everyone else.

If so fortunate as to view him, and near enough to distinguish that it is the hunted fox, think twice before you holloa. More time will be lost than gained by getting their heads up, if the hounds are still on the line, and even when at fault, it is questionable whether they do not derive less assistance than excitement from the human voice. Much depends on circumstances, much on the nature of the pack. I will not say you are never to open your mouth, but I think that if the inmates of our deaf and dumb asylums kept hounds, these would show sport above the average, and would seldom go home without blood. Noise is by no means a necessary concomitant of the chase, and a hat held up, or a quiet whisper to the huntsman, is of more help to him than the loudest and clearest view-holloa that ever wakened the dead "from the lungs of John Peel in the morning."

"The old coachman piloting her children"

RIDING TO FOX-HOUNDS

We have hitherto supposed that you are riding
a good horse, in a good place, and have been so
fortunate as to meet with none of those reverses
that are nevertheless to be expected on occasion,
particularly when hounds run hard and the ground
is deep.   The best of hunters may fall, the boldest
of riders be defeated by an impracticable fence.
Hills, bogs, a precipitous ravine, or even an
unlucky turn in a wood may place you at a mile's
disadvantage, almost before you have realised
your mistake, and you long for the wings of an
eagle, while cursing the impossibility of taking
back so much as a single minute from the past.
It seems so easy to ride a run when it is over !

But do not therefore despair.   Pull yourself
well together, no less than your horse.   Keep
steadily on at a regulated pace, watching the
movements of those who are with the hounds,
and ride inside them, every bend.   No fox goes
perfectly straight—he must turn sooner or later—
and when the happy moment arrives be ready to
back your luck, and *pounce !*   But here, again, I
would have your valour tempered with discretion.
If your horse does not see the hounds, be careful
how you ride him at such large places as he would
face freely enough in the excitement of their
company.   Not one hunter in fifty is really fond
of jumping, and we hardly give them sufficient
credit for the good - humour with which they

accept it as a necessity for enjoyment of the sport. Avoid water especially, unless you have reason to believe the bottom is good, and you can go in and out. Even under such favourable conditions, look well to your egress. There is never much difficulty about the entrance, and do not forget that the middle is often the shallowest, and always the soundest part of a brook. When tempted therefore to take a horse, that you know is a bad water-jumper, at this serious obstacle, you are most likely to succeed if you only ask him to jump half-way. Should he drop his hind legs under the farther bank, he will probably not obtain foothold to extricate himself, particularly with your weight on his back.

We are all panic-stricken, and with reason, at the idea of being submerged, but we might wade through many more brooks than we usually suppose. I can remember seeing the Rowsham, generally believed to be bottomless, forded in perfect safety by half a dozen of the finest and heaviest bullocks the Vale of Aylesbury ever fattened into beef. This, too, close to a hunting-bridge, put there by Baron Rothschild because of the depth and treacherous nature of the stream!

A hard road, however, though to be avoided religiously when enjoying a good place with hounds, is an invaluable ally on these occasions of discomfiture and vexation, if it leads in the same direction as the line of chase. On its firm, unyielding surface your horse is regaining his wind with every stride. Should a turnpike-gate bar your progress, chuck the honest fellow a shilling who swings it back and never mind the change. We hunt on sufferance; for our own sakes we cannot make the amusement too popular with the lower classes. The same argument holds good as to feeing a countryman who assists you in any way when you have a red coat on your back. Reward him with an open hand. He will go to the public-house and drink "fox-hunting" amongst his friends. It is impossible to say how many innocent cubs are preserved by such judicious liberality to die what Charles Payne calls "a natural death."

And now your quiet perseverance meets its reward. You regain your place with the hounds, and are surprised to find how easily and temperately your horse, not yet exhausted, covers large flying fences in his stride. A half-beaten hunter, as I have already observed, will "lob over" high and wide places if they can be done in a single effort, although instinct causes him to "cut them very fine," and forbids unnecessary exertion; but it is "the beginning of the end," and you must not presume on his game, enduring qualities too long.

The object of your pursuit, however, is also mortal. By the time you have tired an honest horse in good condition the fox is driven to his last resources, and even the hounds are less full of fire than when they brought him away from the covert. I am supposing, of course, that they have not changed during the run. You may now save many a furlong by bringing your common-sense into play. What would you do if you were a beaten fox, and where would you go? Certainly not across the middle of those large pastures where you could be seen by the whole troop of your enemies without a chance of shelter or repose. No, you would rather lie down in this deep, overgrown ditch, sneak along the back of that strong, thick bullfinch, turn short in the high, double hedgerow, and so hiding yourself from the spiteful crows that would point you out to the huntsman, try to baffle alike his experienced intelligence and the natural sagacity of his hounds. Such are but the simplest of the wiles practised by this most cunning beast of chase. While observing them, you need no further distress the favourite who has carried you so well than is necessary to render the assistance required for finishing satisfactorily with blood; and here your eyes and ears will be far more useful than the speed and stamina of your horse.

RIDING TO FOX-HOUNDS

Who-whoop! His labours are now over for the day. Do not keep him standing half an hour in the cold, while you smoke a cigar and enlarge to sympathising ears on his doings, and yours, and theirs, and those of everybody concerned. Rather jog gently off as soon as a few compliments and congratulations have been exchanged, and keep him moving at the rate of about six miles an hour, so that his muscles may not begin to stiffen after his violent exertions, till you have got him home. Jump off his honest back, to walk up and down the hills with him as they come. He well deserves this courtesy at your hands. If you ever go out shooting, you cannot have forgotten the relief it is to put down your gun for a minute or two. And even from a selfish point of view, there is good reason for this forbearance in the ease your own frame experiences with the change of attitude and exercise. If you can get him a mouthful of gruel, it will recruit his exhausted vitality, as a basin of soup puts life into a fainting man ; but do not tarry more than five or six minutes for your own luncheon, while he is sucking it in, and the more tired he seems, remember, the sooner you ought to get him home.

If he fails altogether, does not attempt to trot, and wavers from side to side under your weight, put him into the first available shelter, and make up your mind, however mean the quarters, it is better for him to stay there all night than in his exhausted condition to be forced back to his own stable. With thorough ventilation and plenty of coverings, old sacks, blankets, whatever you can lay hands on, he will take no harm. Indeed, if you can keep up his circulation, there is no better restorative than the pure cold air that in a cow-shed, or out-house, finds free admission, to fill his lungs.

You will lose your dinner, perhaps. What matter? You may even have to sleep out in " the worst inn's worst room," unfed, unwashed, and without a change of clothes. It is no such penance after all, and surely your first duty is to the gallant, generous animal that would never fail *you* at your need, but would gallop till his heart broke, for your mere amusement and caprice.

Of all our relations with the dumb creation, there is none in which man has so entirely the best of it as the one-sided partnership that exists between the horse and his rider.

CHAPTER XII

RIDING *AT* STAG-HOUNDS

I HAVE purposely altered the preposition at the heading of this, because it treats of a method so entirely different from that which I have tried to describe in the preceding chapter. At the risk of rousing animadversion from an experienced and scientific majority, I am prepared to affirm that there is nearly as much intelligence and knowledge of the animal required to hunt a deer as a fox, but in following the chase of the larger and higher-scented quadruped there are no fixed rules to guide a rider in his course, so that if he allows the hounds to get out of sight he may gallop over any extent of country till dark, and never hear tidings of them again. Therefore it has been said, one should ride *to* fox-hounds, but *at* stag-hounds, meaning that with the latter, skill and science are of little avail to retrieve a mistake.

Deer, both wild and tame, so long as they are fresh, seem perfectly indifferent whether they run up wind or down, although when exhausted they turn their heads to the cold air that serves to breathe new life into their nostrils. Perhaps, if anything, they prefer to feel the breeze blowing against their sides, but as to this there is no more certainty than in their choice of ground. Other wild animals go to the hill; deer will constantly leave it for the vale. I have seen them fly, straight as an arrow, across a strongly enclosed country, and circle like hares on an open down. Sometimes they will not run a yard till the hounds are at their very haunches; sometimes, when closely pressed, they become stupid with fear, or turn fiercely at bay. " Have we got a good deer to-day?" is a question usually answered with the utmost confidence, yet how often the result is disappointment and disgust. Nor is this the case only in that phase of the sport which may be termed artificial. A wild stag proudly carrying his "brow, bay, and tray" over Exmoor seems no less capricious than an astonished hind, enlarged amongst the brickfields of Hounslow, or the rich pastures that lie outstretched below Harrow-on-the-Hill. One creature, familiar with every inch of its native wastes, will often wander aimlessly in a circle before making its point; the other, not knowing the least where it is bound, will as often run perfectly straight for miles.

My own experience of "the calf," as it has been

ignominiously termed, is limited to three packs—
Mr. Bissett's, who hunts the perfectly wild animal
over the moorlands of Somerset and North Devon ;
Baron Rothschild's, in the Vale of Aylesbury; and
Lord Wolverton's blood - hounds, amongst the
combes of Dorsetshire and "doubles" of the
Blackmoor Vale. With Her Majesty's hounds I
have not been out more than three or four times
in my life.

Let us take the noble chase of the West
country first, as it is followed in glorious autumn
weather through the fairest scenes that ever
haunted a painter's dream ; in Horner woods and
Cloutsham Ball, over the grassy slopes of Exmoor,
and across the broad expanse of Brendon, spread-
ing its rich mantle of purple under skies of gold.
We could dwell for pages on the associations
connected with such classical names as Badge-
worthy-water, New-Invention, Mountsey Gate, or
wooded Glenthorne, rearing its garlanded brows
above the Severn sea. But we are now concerned
in the practical question, how to keep a place with
Mr. Bissett's six-and-twenty-inch hounds running
a warrantable deer over the finest scenting country
in the world?

You may ride *at* them as like a tailor as you
please. The ups and downs of a Devonshire
combe will soon put you in your right place, and
you will be grateful for the most trifling hint that

helps you to spare your horse, and remain on any kind of terms with them, on ground no less trying to his temper and intelligence than to his wind and muscular powers.

Till you attempt to gallop alongside, you will hardly believe how hard the hounds are running. They neither carry such a head, nor dash so eagerly, I might almost say jealously, for the scent as if they were hunting their natural quarry, the fox. This difference I attribute to the larger size, and consequently stronger odour, of a deer. Every hound enjoying his full share, none are tempted to rob their comrades of the mysterious pleasure, and we therefore miss the quick, sharp turns and the *drive* that we are accustomed to consider so characteristic of the fox-hound. They string, too, in long-drawn line, because of the tall, bushy heather, necessitating great size and power, through which they must make their way; but, nevertheless, they keep swinging steadily on, without a check or hover, for many a mile of moorland, showing something of that fierce indomitable perseverance attributed by Byron to the wolf—

"With his long gallop that can tire
The hound's deep hate and hunter's fire."

If you had a second Eclipse under you, and rode him fairly with them, yard for yard, you would stop him in less than twenty minutes!

RIDING *AT* STAG-HOUNDS

Yet old practitioners, notably that prince of sportsmen, the Rev. John Russell, contrive to see runs of many hours' duration without so entirely exhausting their horses but that they can travel some twenty miles home across the moor. Such men as Mr. Granville Somerset, the late Mr. Dene of Barnstaple, Mr. Bissett himself, though weighing twenty stone, and a score of others—for in the West good sportsmen are the rule, not the exception—go well from find to finish of these long, exhausting chases, yet never trespass too far on the generosity and endurance of the noble animal that carries them to the end. And why? Because they take pains, use their heads sagaciously, their hands skilfully, and their heels scarcely at all. To their experience I am indebted for the following little hints which I have found serviceable when embarked on those wide, trackless wastes, brown, endless, undulating, and spacious as the sea.

There are happily no fences, and the chief obstructions to be defeated, or rather negotiated, are the "combes"—a succession of valleys that trend upward from the shallow streams to the heathery ridges, narrowing as they ascend till lost in the level surface of the moor. Never go down into these until your deer is sinking. So surely as you descend will you have to climb the opposite rise; rather keep round them towards the top, watching the hounds while they thread a thousand intricacies of rock, heather, and scattered copse-wood, so as to meet them when they emerge, which they will surely do on the upper level, for it is the nature of their quarry to rise the hill a-slant, and seek safety, when pressed, in its speed across the flat.

A deer descends these declivities one after another as they come, but it is for the refreshment of a bath in their waters below, and instinct prompts it to return without delay to higher ground when thus invigorated. Only if completely beaten and exhausted, does it become so confused as to attempt scaling a rise in a direct line. The run is over then, and you may turn your horse's head to the wind, for in a furlong or two the game will falter and come down again amongst its pursuers to stand at bay.

Coast your combes, therefore, judiciously, and spare your horse; so shall you cross the heather in thorough enjoyment of the chase till it leads you perhaps to the grassy swamps of Exmoor, the most plausible line in the world, over which hounds run their hardest—and now look out!

If Exmoor were in Leicestershire, it would be called a bog, and cursed accordingly, but every country has its own peculiarities, and a North Devon sportsman more especially, on a horse whose dam, or even grandam, was bred on the

"While you smoke a cigar"

moor, seems to flap his way across it with as much confidence as a bittern or a curlew. Could I discover how he accomplished this feat I would tell you, but I can only advise you to ride his line and follow him yard for yard.

There are certain sound tracks and pathways, no doubt, in which a horse does not sink more than fetlock deep, and Mr. Knight, the lord of the soil, may be seen, on a large handsome thorough-bred hunter, careering away as close to the pack as he used to ride in the Vale of Aylesbury, but for a stranger so to presume would be madness, and if he did not find himselt bogged in half a minute, he would stop his horse in half a mile.

Choose a pilot then, Mr. Granville Somerset we will say, or one of the gentlemen I have already named, and stick to him religiously till the welcome heather is brushing your stirrup-irons once more. On Brendon, you may ride for yourself with perfect confidence in the face of all beholders, bold and conspicuous as Dunkery Beacon, but on Exmoor you need not be ashamed to play follow my leader. Only give him room enough to fall!

As, although a full-grown or warrantable stag is quickly found, the process of separating it from its companions, called " tufting," is a long business, lasting for hours, you will be wise to take with you a feed of corn and a rope halter, the latter of which greatly assists in serving your horse with the former. You will find it also a good plan to have your saddles previously well stuffed and repaired, lined with smooth linen. The weather in August is very hot, and your horse will be many hours under your weight, therefore it is well to guard against a sore back. Jump off, too, whenever you have the chance ; a hunter cannot but find it a delightful relief to get rid of twelve or thirteen stone bumping all day against his spine for a minute or two at a time. I have remarked, however, with some astonishment, that the heavier the rider the more averse he seems to granting this indulgence, and am forced to suppose his unwillingness to get down proceeds, as my friend Mr. Grimston says, from a difficulty in getting up again! This gentleman, however, who, notwithstanding his great weight, has always ridden perfectly straight to hounds, over the stiffest of grass countries, obstinately declines to leave the saddle at any time under less provocation than a complete turn - over by the strength of a gate or stile.

To mention "the Honourable Robert" brings one by an irresistible association of ideas into the wide pastures of that grassy paradise which mortals call the Vale of Aylesbury. Here, under the excellent management of Sir Nathaniel

Rothschild, assisted by his brother Mr. Leopold, the carted deer is hunted on the most favourable terms, and a sportsman must indeed be prejudiced who will not admit that ten-mile points over grass with one of the handsomest packs of hounds in the world, are most enjoyable; the object of chase, when the fun is over, returning to Mentmore, like a gentleman, in his own carriage, notwithstanding.

Fred Cox is the picture of a huntsman. Mark Howcott, his whip, fears nothing in the shape of a fence, and will close with a wicked stag, in or out of water, as readily as a policeman collars a pickpocket! The horses are superb, and so they ought to be, for the fences that divide this grazing district into fields of eighty and a hundred acres grow to the most formidable size and strength. Unless brilliantly mounted, neither masters nor servants could hold the commanding position through a run that they always seem to desire.

In riding to these hounds, as to all others, it is advisable to avoid the crowd. Many of the hedgerows are double, with a ditch on each side, and to wait for your turn amongst a hundred horsemen, some too bold, some too cautious, would entail such delay as must prove fatal with a good scent. Happily, there are plenty of gates, and a deer preferring timber to any other leap, usually selects this convenient mode of transit.

Should they be chained, look for a weak place in the fence, which, being double, will admit of subdividing your leap by two, and your chance of a fall by ten.

At first you may be somewhat puzzled on entering a field to find your way out. I will suppose that in other countries you have been accustomed to select the easiest place at once in the fence you are approaching, and to make for it without delay, but across these large fields the nature of an obstacle deceives your eye. The two contiguous hedges that form one boundary render it very difficult to determine at a distance where the easiest place *is*, so you will find it best to follow the hounds, and take your chance. The deer, like your horse, is a large quadruped, and, except under unusual circumstances, where one goes the other can probably follow.

This, I fear, is a sad temptation to ride on the line of hounds. If you give way to it, let the whole pack be at least two or three hundred yards in front, and beware, even then, of tail hounds coming up to join their comrades.

Be careful, also, never to jump a fence in your stride, till you see the pack well into the next field. A deer is very apt to drop lightly over a wall or upright hedge just high enough to conceal it, and then turn short at a right angle under this convenient screen. It would be painful to realise

RIDING *AT* STAG-HOUNDS

your feelings, poised in air over eight or ten couple of priceless hounds, with a chorus of remonstrances storming in the rear! It is no use protesting you "Didn't touch them," you "Didn't mean it," you "Never knew they were there." Better ride doggedly on, over the largest places you can find, and apologise humbly to everybody at the first check.

When a fox goes down to water he means crossing, not so the deer. If at all tired, or heated, it may stay there for an hour. On such occasions, therefore, you can take a pull at your horse and your flask too if you like, while you look for the best way to the other side. When induced to leave it, however, the animal seems usually so refreshed by its bath as to travel a long distance, and on this, as on many other occasions in stag-hunting, the run seems only beginning, when you and your horse consider it ought to be nearly over.

Directly you observe a deer, that has hitherto gone straight, describing a series of circles, you may think about going home.

It is tired at last, and will give you no more fun for a month. You should offer assistance to the men, and, even if it be not accepted, remain, as a matter of courtesy, to see your quarry properly taken, and sent back to the paddock in its cart.

With all stag-hounds, the same rules would seem to apply. Never care to view it, and above all, unless expressly requested to do so for a reason, avoid the solecism of " riding the deer." On the mode in which this sport is conducted depends the whole difference between a wild exhilarating pastime and a tame uninteresting parade. Though prejudice will not allow it is the *real* thing, we cannot but admit the excellence of the imitation, and a man must possess a more logical mind, a less excitable temperament, than is usually allotted to sportsmen, who can remember, while sailing along with hounds running hard over a flying country, that he is only " trying to catch what he had already," and has turned a handsome hairy-coated quadruped out of a box for the mere purpose of putting it in again when the fun is over !

Follow every turn then religiously, and with good intent. You came out expressly to enjoy a gallop, do not allow yourself to be disappointed. If nerve and horse are good enough, go into every field with them, but, I entreat you, ride like a sportsman, and give the hounds plenty of room.

This last injunction more especially applies to that handsome pack of black-and-tans with which Lord Wolverton, during the last five or six seasons, has shown extraordinary sport for the amusement of his neighbours on the uplands of

"A mouthful of gruel"

RIDING *AT* STAG-HOUNDS

Dorset and in the green pastures that enrich the valley of the Stour. These blood-hounds, for such they are, and of the purest breed, stand seven or eight-and-twenty inches, with limbs and frames proportioned to so gigantic a stature. Their heads are magnificent, solemn sagacious eyes, pendent jowls, and flapping ears that brush away the dew. Thanks to his lordship's care in breeding, and the freedom with which he has drafted, their feet are round, and their powerful legs symmetrically straight. A spirited and truly artistic picture of these hounds in chase, sweeping like a whirlwind over the downs, by Mr. Goddard, the well-known painter, hangs on Lord Wolverton's staircase in London, and conveys to his guests, particularly after dinner, so vivid an idea of their picturesque and even sporting qualities as I cannot hope to represent with humble pen and ink.

One could almost fancy, standing opposite this masterpiece, that one heard the cry. Full, sonorous, and musical, it is not extravagant to compare these deep-mouthed notes with the peal of an organ in a cathedral.

Yet they run a tremendous pace. Stride, courage, and condition (the last essential requiring constant care) enable them to sustain such speed over the open as can make a good horse look foolish! While, amongst enclosures, they charge the fences in line, like a squadron of heavy dragoons.

Yet for all this fire and mettle in chase, they are sad cowards under pressure from a crowd. A whip cracked hurriedly, a horse galloping in their track, even an injudicious rate, will make the best of them shy and sulky for half the day. Only by thorough knowledge of his favourites, and patient deference to their prejudices, has Lord Wolverton obtained their confidence, and it is wonderful to mark how his perseverance is rewarded. While he hunts them they are perfectly handy, and turn like a pack of harriers ; but if an outsider attempts to "cap them on," or otherwise interfere, they decline to acknowledge him from the first ; and should they be left to his guidance, are quite capable of going straight home at once, with every mark of contempt.

In a run, however, their huntsman is seldom wanting. His lordship has an extraordinary knack of galloping, getting across a field with surprising quickness on every horse he rides, and is not to be turned by the fence when he reaches it, so that his hounds are rarely placed in the awkward position of a pack at fault with no one to look to for assistance. He has acquired, too, considerable familiarity with the habits of his game, and has a holy horror of going home without it, so perseveres, when at a loss, through many a long hour of cold hunting, slotting, scouring the country for information, and other drawbacks to enjoyment of his chase. As he says himself, " The worst of a deer is, you can't leave off when you like. Nobody will believe you if you swear it went to ground ! "

Part of the country in his immediate neighbour-hood seems made for stag-hunting. Large fields, easy slopes, light fences, and light land, with here and there a hazel copse, bordering a stretch for three or four miles of level turf, like Launceston Down, or Blandford racecourse, must needs tempt a deer to go straight no less than a horseman ; but the animal, as I have said, is unaccountably capricious, and if we could search his lordship's diary I believe we should find his best runs have taken place over a district differing in every respect from the above.

As soon as the leaves are fallen sufficiently to render the Blackmoor Vale rideable, it is his greatest pleasure to take the blood-hounds down to those deep, level, and strongly-enclosed pastures, over which, notwithstanding the size and nature of the fences, he finds his deer (usually hinds) run remarkably well, and make extraordinary points. Ten miles, on the ordnance map, is no unusual distance, and is often accomplished in little more than an hour. For men who enjoy *riding* I can conceive no better fun. Not an acre of plough is to be seen. The enclosures, perhaps, are rather small, but this only necessitates more jumping, and the fences may well satisfy the hungriest, or as an Irishman would say, the *thirstiest*, of competitors! They are not, however, quite so formidable as they look. To accomplish two blind ditches, with a bank between, and a hedge thereon, requires indeed discretion in a horse, and cool determination in its rider, but where these exist the large leap is divided easily by two, and a good man, who means going, is not often to be pounded, even in the Blackmoor Vale.

Nothing is *quite* perfect under the sun, not your own best hunter, nor your wife's last baby, and the river Stour, winding through them in every direction, somewhat detracts from the merit of these happiest of hunting-grounds. A good friend to the deer, and a sad hindrance to its pursuers, it has spoilt many a fine run; but even with this drawback there are few districts in any part of England so naturally adapted to the pleasures of the chase. The population is scanty, the countrymen are enthusiasts, the farmers the best fellows on earth, the climate seems unusually favourable; from the kindness and courtesy of Sir Richard Glynn and Mr. Portman, who pursue the *legitimate* sport over the same locality, and his own personal popularity, the normal difficulties of his undertaking are got over in favour of the

noble master, and everybody seems equally
pleased to welcome the green plush coats and
the good grey horses in the midst of the
black-and-tans.

If I were sure of a fine morning and a safe
mount, I would ask for no keener pleasure than
an hour's gallop with Lord Wolverton's blood-
hounds over the Blackmoor Vale.

CHAPTER XIII

THE PROVINCES

A DISTINGUISHED soldier of the present day, formerly as daring and enthusiastic a rider as ever charged his "oxers" with the certainty of a fall, was once asked in my hearing by a mild stranger, "Whether he had been out with the Crawley and Horsham?" if I remember right.

"No, sir!" was the answer, delivered in a tone that somewhat startled the querist, "I have never hunted with any hounds in my life but the Quorn and the Pytchley, and I'll take d—d good care I never do!"

Now I fancy that not a few of our "golden youth," who are either born to it, or have contrived in their own way to get the "silver spoon" into their mouths, are under the impression that all hunting must necessarily be dead slow if conducted out of Leicestershire, and that little sport, with less excitement, is to be obtained in those remote regions which they contemptuously term the provinces.

THE PROVINCES

There never was a greater fallacy. If we calculate the number of hours hounds are out of kennel (for we must remember that the Quorn and Belvoir put two days into one), we shall find, I think, that they run hard for fewer minutes, in proportion, across the fashionable countries than in apparently less-favoured districts concealed at sundry out-of-the-way corners of the kingdom.

Nor is this disparity difficult to understand. Fox-hunting at its best is a wild sport; the wilder the better. Where coverts are many miles apart, where the animal must travel for its food, where agriculture is conducted on primitive principles that do not necessitate the huntsman's horror, "a man in every field," the fox retains all his savage nature, and is prepared to run any distance, face every obstacle, rather than succumb to his relentless enemy, the hound. He has need, and he seems to know it, of all his courage and all his sagacity, as compelled to fight alone on his own behalf, without assistance from that invaluable ally, the crowd.

A score of hard riders, nineteen of whom are jealous, and the twentieth determined not to be beat, forced on by a hundred comrades all eager for the view and its stentorian proclamation, may well save the life of any fox on earth, with scarce an effort from the animal itself. But that hounds are creatures of habit, and huntsmen in the flying countries miracles of patience, no less than their masters, not a nose would be nailed on the kennel-door, after cub-hunting was over, from one end of the shires to the other.

Nothing surprises me so much as to see a pack of hounds, like the Belvoir or the Quorn, come up through a crowd of horses and stick to the line of their fox, or fling gallantly forward to recover it, without a thought of personal danger or the slightest misgiving that not one man in ten is master of the two pair of hoofs beneath him, carrying death in every shoe. Were they not bred for the make-and-shape that gives them speed no less than for fineness of nose, but especially for that *dash* which, like all victorious qualities, leaves something to chance, they could never get a field from the covert. It does happen, however, that, now and again, a favourable stroke of fortune puts a couple of furlongs between the hounds and their pursuers. A hundred-acre field of well saturated grass lies before them, down go their noses, out go their sterns, and away they scour, at a pace which makes a precious example of young Rapid on a first-class steeplechase horse with the wrong bridle in his mouth.

But how differently is the same sport being carried out in his father's country, perhaps by the old gentleman's own pack, with which the young one considers it slow to hunt.

THE PROVINCES

Let us begin at the beginning and try to imagine a good day in the provinces, about the third week in November, when leaves are thin and threadbare on the fences, while copse and woodland glisten under subdued shafts of sunlight in sheets of yellow gold.

What says Mr. Warburton, favoured of Diana and the Muses?

> " The dew-drop is clinging
> To whin-bush and brake,
> The sky-lark is singing,
> Merry hunters, awake!
> Home to the cover,
> Deserted by night,
> The little red rover
> Is bending his flight—"

Could words more stirringly describe the hope and promise, the joy, the vitality, the buoyant exhilaration of a hunting morning?

So the little red rover, who has travelled half a dozen miles for his supper, returns to find he has "forgotten his latchkey," and curls himself up in some dry, warm nook amongst the brushwood, at the quietest corner of a deep, precipitous ravine.

Here, while sleep favours digestion, he makes himself very comfortable, and dreams, no doubt, of his own pleasures and successes in pursuit of prey. Presently, about half-past eleven, he wakes with a start, leaps out of bed, shakes his fur, and

213

stands to listen, a perfect picture, with one pad raised and his cunning head a-slant. Yes, he recognised it from the first. The "Yooi, wind him, and rouse him!" of old Matthew's mellow tones, not unknown in a gin-and-water chorus when occasion warrants the convivial brew, yet clear, healthy, and resonant as the very roar of Challenger, who has just proclaimed his consciousness of the drag, some five hours old.

'Tis an experienced rover, and does not hesitate for an instant. Stealing down the ravine, he twists his agile little body through a tangled growth of blackthorn and brambles, crosses the stream dry-footed with a leap, and, creeping through the fence that bounds his stronghold, peers into the meadow beyond. No smart and busy whip has "clapped forward" to view and head him. Matthew, indeed, brings out but one, and swears he could do better without *him*. So the rover puts his sharp nose straight for the solitude he loves, and whisking his brush defiantly, resolves to make his point.

He has been gone five minutes when the clamour of the find reaches his ears, twice that time ere the hounds are fairly out of covert on his line; so, with a clear head and a bold heart, he has leisure to consider his tactics and to remember the main earth at Crag's-end in the forest, twelve miles off as the crow flies.

"Poised in air"

THE PROVINCES

Challenger, and Charmer his progeny, crash out of the wood together, fairly howling with ecstasy as their busy noses meet the rich tufted herbage, dewy, dank, and tainted with the maddening odour that affords such uncontrolled enjoyment. "Harve art him, my lards!" exclaims old Matthew, in Doric accents, peculiar to the kennel. "Come up, horse!" and, having admonished that faithful servant with a dig in the ribs from his horn, blows half a dozen shrill blasts in quick succession, sticks the instrument, I shudder to confess it, in his boot, and proceeds to hustle his old white nag at the best pace he can command in the wake of his favourites. "Dang it! they're off," exclaims a farmer, who had stationed himself on the crest of the hill, diving, at a gallop, down a stony darkling lane, overgrown with alder, brambles, honeysuckle, all the garden produce of uncultivated nature, lush and steaming in decay. The field, consisting of the Squire, three or four strapping yeomen, a parson, and a boy on a pony, follow his example, and making a good turn in the valley, find themselves splashing through a glittering, shallow streamlet, still in the lane, with the hounds not a bowshot from them on the right.

"And pace?" inquires young Rapid, when his father describes the run to him on Christmas

Eve. "Of course you had no pace with so good a point?"

"Pace, sir!" answers the indignant parent; "my hounds *run* because they can *hunt*. I tell you, they were never off the line for an hour and three-quarters! Matthew *would* try to cast them once, and very nearly lost his fox, but Charmer hit it off on the other side of the combe and put us right. He's as like old Challenger as he can stick; a deal more like than *you* are to *me*."

Young Rapid concedes the point readily, and the Squire continues his narrative: "I had but eighteen couple out, because of a run the week before,—I'll tell you about it presently,—five-and-thirty minutes on the hills, and a kill in the open, that lamed half the pack amongst the flints. You talk of pace—they went fast enough to have settled the best of you, I'll warrant! but I'm getting off the line—I've not done with the other yet. I never saw hounds work better. They came away all together, they hunted their fox like a cluster of bees; swarming over every field, and every fence, they brought him across Tinglebury Tor, where it's always as dry as that hearthstone, through a flock of five hundred sheep, they rattled him in and out of Combe-Bampton, though the Lower Woods were alive with riot—hares, roe, fallow-deer, hang it! apes and peacocks if you like; had old Matthew not been a fool they would never have hesitated for a moment, and when they ran into him under Crag's-end, there wasn't a man-jack of them missing. Not one—that's what I call a pack of hounds!

"The best part of it? So much depends on whether you young fellows go out to hunt, or to ride. For the first half-hour or so we were never off the grass—there's not a ploughed field all the way up the valley till you come to Shifner's allotments, orchard and meadow, meadow and orchard, fetlock-deep in grass, even at this time of year. Why, it carries a side-scent, like the heather on a moor! I suppose you'd have called *that* the best part. I didn't, though I saw it well from the lane with Matthew and the rest of us, all but the Vicar, who went into every field with the hounds — I thought he was rather hard on them amongst those great blind, tangled fences; but he's such a good fellow, I hadn't the heart to holloa at him—it's very wrong, though, and a man in his profession ought to know better.

"I can't say they checked exactly in the allotments, but the manure and rubbish, weeds burning, and what not, brought them to their noses. That's where Matthew made such a fool of himself; but, as I told you, Charmer put us all right. The fox had crossed into Combe-Bampton and was rising the hill for the downs.

"I never saw hounds so patient—they could but just hold a line over the chalk—first one and then another puzzled it out, till they got on better terms in Hazlewood Hanger, and when they ran down into the valley again between the cliffs there was a cry it did one's heart good to hear.

"I had a view of him, crossing Parker's Piece, the long strip of waste land, you know, under Craven Clump; and he seemed as fresh as you are now—I sat as mute as a mouse, for six-and-thirty noses knew better where he'd gone than I did, and six-and-thirty tongues were at work that never told a lie. The Vicar gave them plenty of room by this time, and all our horses seemed to have had about enough!

"'I wish we mayn't have changed in the Hanger,' said Matthew, refreshing the old grey with a side-binder, as they blundered into the lane, but I knew better—he had run the rides, every yard, and that made me hope we should have him in hand before long.

"It began to get very interesting; I was near enough to watch each hound doing his work, eighteen couple, all dogs, three and four season hunters, for I hadn't a single puppy out. I wish you had been there, my boy. It was a real lesson in hunting, and I'll tell you what I thought of them, one by ——. Hulloh! Yes. You'd better ring for coffee—Hanged if I don't believe you've been fast asleep all the time!"

But such runs as these, though wearisome to a listener, are most enjoyable for those who can appreciate the steadiness and sagacity of the hound, no less than the craft and courage of the animal it pursues. There is an indescribable charm, too, in what I may call the romance of hunting,—the remote scenes we should perhaps never visit for their own sake, the broken sunlight glinting through copse and gleaming on fern, the woodland sights, the woodland sounds, the balmy odours of nature, and all the treats she provides for her votaries, tasted and enjoyed, with every faculty roused, every sense sharpened in the excitement of our pursuit. These delights are better known in the provinces than the shires, and to descend from flights of fancy to practical matters of £ s. d., we can hunt in the former at comparatively trifling expense.

In the first place, particularly if good horsemen, we need not be nearly so well mounted. There are few provincial countries in which a man who knows how to ride, cannot get from one field to another, by hook or by crook, with a little creeping and scrambling and blundering, that come far short of the casualty we deprecate as a rattling fall! His horse must be in good condition, of course, and able to gallop; also, if temperate, the more willing at his fences the better, but it is not indispensable that he should possess the stride and power necessary to cover some twenty feet of distance, and four or five of height, at every leap, nor the blood that can alone enable him to repeat the exertion, over and over again, at three-quarter speed in deep ground. To jump, as it is called, from field to field, tries a horse's stamina no less severely than his courage, while, as I have already observed, there is no such economy of effort, and even danger, as to make two small fences out of a large one.

I do not mean to say that there are any parts of England where, if hounds run hard, a hunter, with a workman on his back, has not enough to do to live with them, but I do consider that, *cæteris paribus*, a good rider may smuggle a moderate horse over most of our provincial countries, whereas he would be helpless on the same animal in Leicestershire or Northampton-shire. There, on the other hand, an inferior horseman, bold enough to place implicit confidence in the first-class hunter he rides, may see a run, from end to end, with considerable credit and enjoyment, by the simple process of keeping a good hold of his bridle, while he leaves every-thing to the horse. But he must not have learned a single letter of the noble word "Funk." Directly his heart fails, and he interferes, down they both come, an imperial crowner, and the game is lost!

Many of our provincial districts are also calculated, from their very nature, to turn out experienced sportsmen no less than accomplished riders. In large woods, amongst secluded hills, or wild tracts of moor intersected by impracticable ravines, a lover of the chase is compelled by force of circumstances to depend on his own eyes, ears, and general intelligence for his amusement.

He finds no young Rapid to pilot him over the large places, if he means going; no crafty band of second-horsemen to guide him in safety to the finish, if his ambition is satisfied with a distant and occasional view of the stirring pageant; no convenient hand-gate in the corner, no friendly bridge across the stream; above all, no hurrying cavalcade drawn out for miles, amongst which to hide, and with whom pleasantly to compare notes hereafter in those self-deceiving moments, when

> "Dined, o'er our claret, we talk of the merit,
> Of every choice spirit that rode in the run.
> But here the crowd, Sir, can talk just as loud, Sir,
> As those who were forward enjoying the fun!"

No. In the provinces our young sportsman must make up his mind to take his own part, to study the coverts drawn, and find out for himself the points where he can see, hear, and, so to speak, command hounds till they go away; must learn how to rise the hill with least labour, and descend it with greatest dispatch, how to thread glen, combe, or dale, wind in and out of the rugged ravine, plunge through a morass, and make his way home at night across trackless moor, or open storm-swept down. By the time he has acquired these accomplishments, the horsemanship will have come of itself. He will know how to bore where he cannot jump, to creep where he must not fly, and so manage his horse that the animal seems to share the intentions and intelligence of its rider.

If he can afford it, and likes to spend a season or two in the shires for the last superlative polish, let him go and welcome! He will be taught to get clear of a crowd, to leap timber at short notice, to put on his boots and breeches, and that is about all there is left for him to learn!

In the British army, though more than a hundred regiments constitute the line, each cherishes its own particular title, while applying that general application indiscriminately to the rest.

I imagine the same illusion affects the provinces, and I should offend an incalculable number of good fellows and good sportsmen, were I to describe as *provincial* establishments, the variety of hunts, north, south, east, and west, with which I have enjoyed so much good company and good

fun.   Each has its own claim to distinction, some
have collars, all have sport.

Grass, I imagine, is the one essential that con-
stitutes pre-eminence in a hunting country, and
for this the shires have always boasted they bear
away the palm, but it will surprise many of my
readers to be told that in the south and west there
are districts where this desideratum seems now
more plentiful than in the middle of England.
The Blackmoor Vale still lies almost wholly under
pasture, and you may travel to-day forty miles by
rail, through the counties of Dorset and Somerset,
in general terms nearly from Blandford to Bath,
without seeing a ploughed field.

What a country might here be made by such
an enthusiast as poor "Sam Reynell," who found
Meath without a gorse-covert, and drew between
thirty and forty sure finds in it before he died!

Independently of duty, which ought to be our
first consideration, there is also great convenience
in hunting from home.   We require no large stud,
can choose our meets, and, above all, are indifferent to weather.   A horse comes out so many
times in a season; if we don't hunt to-day, we
shall next week.   Compare this equable frame of
mind with the irritation and impatience of a man
who has ten hunters standing at the sign of "The
Hand-in-Pocket," while he inhabits the front
parlour, without his books, deprived of his usual

society and occupations, the barometer at set fair, and the atmosphere affording every indication of a six-weeks' frost!

Let us see in what the charm consists that impels people to encounter bad food, bad wine, bad lodgings, and above all, protracted boredom, for a campaign in those historical hunting-grounds, that have always seemed to constitute the rosiest illusion of a sportsman's dream.

CHAPTER XIV

THE SHIRES

"Every species of fence every horse doesn't suit,
    What's a good country hunter may here prove a brute,"

SINGS that clerical bard who wrote the
Billesdon-Coplow poem, from which I have
already quoted; and it would be difficult to
explain more tersely than do these two lines the
difference between a fair useful hunter, and the
flyer we call *par excellence* "a Leicestershire
horse!"

Alas! for the favourite unrivalled over
Gloucestershire walls, among Dorsetshire doubles,
in the level ploughs of Holderness, or up and
down the wild Derbyshire hills, when called upon
to gallop, we will say, from Ashby pastures to
the Coplow, after a week's rain, at Quorn pace,
across Quorn fences, unless he happens to possess
with the speed of a steeplechaser, the courage of
a lion and the activity of a cat! For the first
mile or two *pristinæ virtutis haud immemor*
he bears him gallantly enough, even the unaccus-

tomed rail on the far side of an "oxer" elicits but a startling exertion, and a loud rattle of horn and iron against wood, but ere long the slope rises against him, the ridge-and-furrow checks his stride, a field, dotted with ant-hills as large as church-hassocks and not unlike them in shape, to catch his toes and impede his action, changes his smooth easy swing to a laborious flounder, and presently at a thick bullfinch on the crest of a grassy ridge, out of ground that takes him in nearly to his hocks, comes the crisis. Too good a hunter to turn over, he gets his shoulders out and lets his rider see the fall before it is administered, but down he goes notwithstanding, very effectually, to rise again after a struggle, his eye wild, nostril distended, and flanks heaving, thoroughly pumped out!

He is a good horse, but you have brought him into the wrong country, and this is the result.

It would be a hopeless task to extract from young Rapid's laconic phrases, and general indifference, any particulars regarding the burst in which, to give him his due, he has gone brilliantly, or the merits of the horse that carried him in the first flight without a mistake. He wastes his time, his money, his talents, but not his words. For him and his companions, question and answer are cut short somewhat in this wise :—

"Did you get away with them from the Punch-bowl?"

"Yes, I was among the lucky ones."

"Is 'The King of the Golden Mines' any use?"

"I fancy he is good enough."

And yet he is reflecting on the merits of Self and Co. with no little satisfaction, and does not grudge one shilling of the money—a hundred down, and a bill for two hundred and fifty—that the horse with the magnificent name cost him last spring.

Their performance, I admit, does them both credit. I will endeavour to give a rough sketch of the somewhat hazardous amusement that puts him out of conceit with the sport shown by his father's hounds.

Let us picture to ourselves, then, Rapid junior, resplendent in the whitest of breeches and brightest of boots, with a single-breasted, square-cut scarlet coat, a sleek hat curly of brim, four feet of cane hunting-whip in his hand, a flower at his breast, and a toothpick in his mouth, replaced by an enormous cigar as somebody he doesn't know suggests they are not likely to find. Though he looks so helpless, and more than half-asleep, he is wide-awake enough in fact, and dashes the weed unlighted from his lips, when he spies the huntsman stand up in his stirrups as though on the watch. There lurks a fund of latent energy under the placidity of our friend's demeanour, and, as four couple of hounds come streaming out of cover, he shoots up the bank rather too near them, to pick his place without hesitation in an ugly bullfinch at the top. Two of his own kind are making for the same spot at the same moment, and our young friend shows at such a crisis that he knows how to ride. Taking "The King of the Golden Mines" hard by the head, he changes his aim on the instant, and rams the good horse at four feet of strong timber, leaning towards him, with an energy not to be denied. Over they go triumphantly, the King, half affronted, catching hold with some resentment, as he settles vigorously to his stride. What matter? most of the pack are already half-way across the next field, for Leicestershire hounds have an extraordinary knack of flying forward to overtake their comrades. His father would be delighted with the performance, and would call it "scoring to cry," but young Rapid does not trouble himself about such matters. He is only glad to find they are out of his way, and thinks no more about it, except to rejoice that he can put the steam on, without the usual remonstrance from huntsman and master.

The King can gallop like a race-horse, and is soon at the next leap—a wide ditch, a high staked - and - bound hedge, coarse, rough, and strong, with a drop and what you please, on the other side. This last treat proves to be a bowed-out oak - rail, standing four feet from the fence. The King, full of courage and going fast, bounds over the whole with his hind legs tucked under him like a deer, ready, but not requiring, to strike back, while two of Rapid's young friends with whom he dined yesterday, and one he will meet at dinner to-day, fly it in similar form, nearly alongside. An ugly, overgrown bullfinch, with a miniature ravine, or, as it is here called, a bottom, appears at the foot of the hill they are now descending, and, as there seems only one practicable place, these four reckless individuals at once begin to race for the desirable spot. The King's turn of speed serves him again ; covering five or six-and-twenty feet, he leaps it a length in front of the nearest horse, and a couple of strides before the other two, while loud reproach-ful outcries resound in the rear because of Harmony's narrow escape—the King's fore foot missing that priceless bitch by a yard !

Our young gentleman, having got a lead now, begins to ride with more judgment. He trots up to a stile and pops over it in truly artistic form ; better still, he gives the hounds plenty of room on the fallow beyond, where they have hovered for a moment and put down their noses, holding his hand up to warn those behind, a "bit of cheek," as they call this precautionary measure, which he will be made to remember for some days to come!

He is not such a fool but that he knows, from experience in the old country, how a little patience at these critical moments makes the whole difference between a good day's sport and a bad. It would be provoking to lose the chance of a gallop now, when he has got such a start, and is riding the best horse in his stable, so he looks anxiously over his shoulder for the huntsman, who is coming, and stands fifty yards aloof, which he considers a liberal allowance, that the hounds may have space to swing.

To-day there is a good scent and a good fox, a combination that happens oftener than might be supposed. Harmony, who, notwithstanding her recent peril, has never been off the line, though the others over-shot it, scours away at a tangent, with the slightest possible whimper, and her stern down, the leading hounds wheeling to her like pigeons, and the whole pack driving forward again, harder than before.

It is a beautiful turn; young Rapid would admire it, no doubt, were his attention not distracted by the gate out of the field, which is chained up, and a hurried calculation as to whether it is too high for the King to attempt.

The solution is obvious. I need hardly say he

jumps it gallantly in his stride. It would never do, you see, to let those other fellows catch him, and he sails away once more with a stronger lead than at first. What a hunting panorama opens on his view!—a downward stretch of a couple of miles, and a gentle rise beyond of more than twice that distance, consisting wholly of enormous grass fields, dotted here and there with single trees, and separated by long lines of fences, showing black and level on that faded expanse of green. The smoke from a farmhouse rises white and thin against the dull sky in the middle distance, and a taper church-spire points to heaven from behind the hill, otherwise there is not an object for miles to recall everyday life ; and young Rapid's world consists at this moment of two reeking pointed ears, with a vision of certain dim shapes, fleeting like shadows across the open—swift, dusky, and noiseless as a dream.

His blood thrills with excitement, from the crown of his close-cropped head to his silken-covered heel ; but education is stronger than nature, and he tightens his lips, perhaps to repress a cheer, while he murmurs—"Over the brook for a hundred! and the King never turned from water in his life."

Two more fences bring him to the level meadow with its willows. Harmony is shaking herself on the farther bank, and he has marked

RIDING RECOLLECTIONS

with his eye the spot where he means to take off.
A strong pull, a steady hand, the energy of a
mile gallop condensed into a dozen strides, and
the stream passes beneath him like a flash. "It's
a rum one!" he murmurs, standing up in his
stirrups to ease the good horse, while one follower
exclaims "Bravo! Rapid. Go along, old man!"
as the speaker plunges overhead; and another,
who lands with a scramble, mutters, "D—n him,
I shall never catch him! my horse is done to a
turn *now*."

The King, his owner thinks, is well worth the
£350 that has *not* been paid. The horse has
caught his second wind, and keeps striding on,
strong and full of running, though temperate
enough now, and, in such a country as this, a
truly delightful mount.

There is no denying that our friend is a capital
horseman, and bold as need be. "The King of
the Golden Mines," with a *workman* on his back,
can hardly be defeated by any obstacle that the
power and spring of a quadruped ought to surmount. He has tremendous stride, and no less
courage than his master, so fence after fence is
thrown behind the happy pair with a sensation
like flying, that seems equally gratifying to both.
The ground is soft but sound enough; the leaps,
though large, are fair and clean. One by one
they are covered in light, elastic bounds, of

232

eighteen or twenty feet, and for a mile, at least, the King scarcely alters his action, and never changes his leg. Young Rapid would ask no better fun than to go on like this for a week.

Once he has a narrow escape. The fox having turned short up a hedgerow after crossing it, the hounds, though running to kill, turn as short, for which they deserve the praise there is nobody present to bestow, and Rapid, charging the fence with considerable freedom, just misses landing in the middle of the pack. I know it, because he acknowledged it after dinner, professing, at the same time, devout thankfulness that master and huntsman were too far off to see. Just such another turn is made at the next fence, but this time on the near side. The hounds disappear suddenly, tumbling over each other into the ditch like a cascade. Peering between his horse's ears, the successful rider can distinguish only a confused whirl of muddy backs, and legs, and sterns, seen through a cloud of steam ; but smothered growls, with a certain vibration of the busy cluster, announce that they have got him, and Rapid so far forgets himself as to venture on a feeble " Who-whoop ! "

Before he can leap from the saddle the huntsman comes up, followed by two others, one of whom, pulling out his watch, with a delighted face repeats frantically, " Seven-and-twenty minutes, and a kill in the open! *What* a good gallop! Not the ghost of a check from end to end. Seven-and-twenty minutes," and so on, over and over again.

While the field straggle in, and the obsequies of this good fox are properly celebrated, a little enthusiasm would be justifiable enough on the part of a young gentleman who has had the best of it unquestionably through the whole of so brilliant a scurry. He might be expected to enlarge volubly, and with excusable self-conscious-ness, on the pace, the country, the straight running of the fox, the speed and gallantry of the hounds; nor could we blame him for praising by implica-tion his own determined riding in a tribute to " The King of the Golden Mines."

But such extravagancies are studiously re-pudiated and repressed by the school to which young Rapid belongs. All he *does* say is this—

" I wonder when the second horses will come up? I want some luncheon before we go and find another fox."

I have already observed that in the shires we put two days into one. Where seventy or eighty couple of hounds are kept and thirty horses, to hunt four times a week, with plenty of country, in which you may find a fox every five minutes, there can be no reason for going home while light serves; and really good scenting days occur so rarely that we may well be tempted to make the most of one even with jaded servants and a half-tired pack of hounds. The field, too, are considerably diminished by three or four o'clock. One has no second horse, another must get home to write his letters, and, if within distance of Melton, some hurry back to play whist. Everything is comparative. With forty or fifty horsemen left, a huntsman breathes more freely, and these, who are probably enthusiasts, begin to congratulate themselves that the best of the day is yet to come. "Let us go and draw Melton Spinney," is a suggestion that brightens every eye; and the Duke will always draw Melton Spinney so long as he can see. It is no unusual thing for his hounds to kill, and, I have been told, they once *found* their fox by moonlight, so that it is proverbial all over his country, if you only stop out late enough, you are sure of a run with the Belvoir at last. And then, whether you belong to the school of young Rapid or his father, you will equally have a treat. Are you fond of hounds? Here is a pack that cannot be surpassed, to delight the most fastidious eye, satisfy the most critical taste. Do you like to see them hunt? Watch how these put their noses down, tempering energy with patience, yet so bustling and resolute as to work a bad scent into a good one. Are you an admirer of make-

and-shape ? Mark this perfect symmetry of form, bigger, stronger, and tougher than it looks. Do you understand kennel management and condition ? Ask Gillard why his hounds are never known to tire, and get from him what hints you can.

Lastly, do you want to gallop and jump, defeat your dearest friends, and get to the end of your best horse ? That is but a moderate scenting day on which the Belvoir will not afford opportunity to do both. If you can live with them while they run, and see them race into their fox at the finish, I congratulate you on having science, nerve, all the qualities of horsemanship, a good hunter, and, above all, a good groom.

These remarks as to pace, stoutness, and sporting qualities, apply also to the Quorn, the Cottesmore, and the Pytchley. This last, indeed, with its extensive range of woodlands in Rockingham Forest, possesses the finest hunting country in England, spacious enough to stand six days a week in the mildest of winters all the season through. Under the rule of Lord Spencer, who has brought to bear on his favourite amusement the talent, energy, and administrative powers that, while they remained in office, were so serviceable to his party, the Pytchley seems to have recovered its ancient renown, and the sport provided for the white collars during the last year or two has been much above the average.

236

THE SHIRES

His lordship thoroughly understands the whole
management of hounds, in the kennel and the
field, is enthusiastically fond of the pursuit, and,
being a very determined rider as well as an
excellent judge of a horse, is always present
in an emergency to observe the cause and take
measures for the remedy. Will Goodall has but
little to learn as a huntsman, and, like his father,
the unrivalled Will Goodall of Belvoir celebrity,
places implicit confidence in his hounds. "They
can put me right," seems his maxim, "oftener
than I can put them!" If a man wanted to see
a gallop in the shires at its best, he should meet
the Pytchley some Saturday in February at
Waterloo Gorse, but I am bound to caution him
that he ought to ride a brilliant hunter, and, as
young Rapid would say, "harden his heart" to
make strong use of him.

Large grass fields, from fifty to a hundred
acres in extent, carrying a rare scent, are indeed
tempting; but to my own taste, though perhaps
in this my reader may not agree with me, they
would be more inviting were they not separated
by such forbidding fences. A high blackthorn
hedge, strong enough to hold an elephant, with
one, and sometimes two ditches, fortified, moreover, in many cases, by a rail placed half a horse's
length off to keep out cattle from the thorns,
offers, indeed, scope for all the nobler qualities of

237

man and beast, but while sufficiently perilous for glory, seems to my mind rather too stiff for pleasure!

And yet I have seen half a dozen good men well mounted live with hounds over this country for two or three miles on end without a fall, nor do I believe that in these stiffly-fenced grazing grounds the average of dirty coats is greater than in less difficult-looking districts. It may be that those who compete are on the best of hunters, and that a horse finds all his energies roused by the formidable nature of such obstacles, if he means to face them at all!

And now a word about those casualties which perhaps rather enhance than damp our ardour in the chase.

Mr. Assheton Smith used to say that no man could be called a good rider who did not *know how to fall*. Founded on his own exhaustive experience, there is much sound wisdom in this remark. The oftener a man is down, the less likely is he to be hurt, and although, as the old joke tells us, absence of body as regards danger seems even preferable to presence of mind, the latter quality is not without its advantage in the crisis that can no longer be deferred.

I have seen men so flurried when their horses' noses touched the ground as to fling themselves wildly from the saddle, and meet their own

THE SHIRES

apprehensions half-way, converting an uncertain scramble into a certain downfall. Now it should never be forgotten that a horse in difficulties has the best chance of recovery if the rider sits quiet in the middle of his saddle and lets the animal's head alone. It is always time enough to part company when his own knee touches the ground, and as he then knows exactly *where* his horse is, he can get out of the way of its impending body, ere it comes heavily to the earth. If his seat is not strong enough to admit of such desirable tenacity, let him at least keep a firm hold of the bridle; that connecting link will, so to speak, preserve his communications, and a kick with one foot, or timely roll of his own person, will take him out of harm's way.

The worst fall a man can get is to be thrown over his horse's head, with such violence as to lay him senseless till the animal, turning a somersault, crushes his prostrate body with all the weight of its own. Such accidents must sometimes happen, of course, but they are not necessarily of everyday occurrence. By riding with moderate speed at his fences, and preserving, on all occasions, coolness, good-humour, and confidence in his partner, a sportsman, even when past his prime, may cross the severest parts of the Harborough country itself with an infinitesimal amount of danger to life and limb. Kind-

ness, coercion, hand, seat, valour, and discretion
should be combined in due proportion, and the
mixture, as far as the hunting-field is concerned,
will come out a real *elixir vitæ* such as the pale
Rosicrucian poring over crucible and alembic
sought to compound in vain.

I cannot forbear quoting once more from the
gallant soul-stirring lines of Mr. Bromley
Davenport, himself an enthusiast who, to this
day, never seems to remember he has a neck
to break!

"What is time? the effusion of life zoophytic,
 In dreary pursuit of position or gain.
What is life? the absorption of vapours mephitic,
 The bursting of sunlight on senses and brain.
Such a life has been mine, though so speedily over,
 Condensing the joys of a century's course,
From the find, till they ate him near Woodwell-Head Covert,
 In thirty bright minutes from Banksborough Gorse!"

Yes, when all is said and done, perhaps the
very acme and perfection of a *riding* run, is
to be attained within fifteen miles of Melton.
A man who has once been fortunate enough
to find himself, for ever so short a distance,
leading

"The cream of the cream, in the shire of shires,"

will never, I imagine, forget his feelings of
triumph and satisfaction while he occupied so
proud a position; nor do I think that, as a

THE SHIRES

matter of mere amusement and pleasurable excitement, life can offer anything to compare with a good horse, a good conscience, a good start, and

"A quick thirty minutes from Banksborough Gorse."

THE END

INDEX

INDEX

D

Davenport, Bromley, quoted, 180, 240.
Day's run in the provinces, 213 *seq*.
Deer—
    Capricious, 207.
    Describing series of circles, 203.
    Going to water, 203.
Dene, of Barnstaple, stag-hunting, 197.
Discretion, 119 *seq*.
Dorsetshire farmer's system of teaching timber-jumping, 7.
Double-bridle, 38.
Dunchurch double-bridles, Nos. 1 and 2, 54.
Dunkery Beacon, 199.
Dwyer, Major, bridle, 54.

E

Eclipse, 196.
Elgin Marbles, Greek riders, 35.
    Without stirrups, 92.
Exmoor characteristics, 198.
Exmoor pony in bog, 4.

F

Fairfax, on bridle, 33.
Falls, 239.
Fellowes, of Shottisham, riding at timber, 22.
Fences in Pytchley country, 237.
Firr, Tom, leaping, 76.
Fordham on use of spurs, 56.
Fox—
    Going to water, 203.
    Travelling down wind, 175.
    Wiles practised by, 190.
Fox-hounds, riding to, 171 *seq*.
    Anticipating a check, 185.
    Hard roads, when useful, 188.
    Hounds quartering their ground, 181.

Fox-hounds, riding to, *contd.*—
    Huntsman's horse, work done by, 182.
    Huntsman's pilotage to be followed, 173.
    Intuitive perception of "line of chase," 176.
    Judicious choice of ground essential, 178.
    Keeping near hounds, 171, 181.
    Old sportsman's advice, 183.
    Returning after run, advice on, 191.
    "Riding on their line," 175.
    Start, advice on, 172.
    Viewing fox, 185, 186.
    Water to be avoided, 188.
    Wild sport, 211.
Fraser, Colonel, horsemanship, 17.
Froissart, knights in saddle, 90.

G

Gag, 48.
Gardner, Lord, approval of Major Dwyer's bridle, 54.
Gardner, Lord, leap over rails, 110.
George IV., opinion of Colonel Wyndham, 128.
Gillard, 236.
Gilmour, not using spurs, 62.
Gilmour, riding at timber, 22.
Gilmour's *Vingt-et-un*, 162.
Glynn, Sir Richard, 208.
Goddard, picture of Lord Wolverton's hounds, 205.
Goodall, Will, senior and junior, 237.
Grass, where found, 223.
Greaves, Mackenzie, horsemanship, 51, 86.
Greenwood, Colonel, illustration of riding, 51.
    Hunting with single curb-bridle, 6.
Grey, Lord, riding at timber, 22.
Grimston, on dismounting, 200.
Gurney, Richard, on "Sober Robin," 169.

INDEX

H

Hand, 68 *seq.*
 A gift, not an acquirement, 69.
 Qualities comprised under, 68, 80, 82, 88.
Harborough country, 239.
"Hard Bargain," 55.
Hare - hunting as school for thorough-breds, 165.
Head, Sir Francis, on danger in battle and hunting, 105, 113.
Holderness, level ploughs of, 225.
Horses—
 Accommodate themselves to rider who subjugates *one*, 16.
 "Boring," 48.
 Discretion most valuable quality in, 135.
 Docile nature, 40.
 Eastern, broken with severe bits, 45.
 Game qualities of English, 158.
 Good understanding between rider and, 16.
 Habit of obedience, 6, 14.
 Hack, advice on hunting on, 121.
 Intellect to be cultivated, 4.
 "Leicestershire horse," 225.
 Mechanical, in Piccadilly, 93 *seq.*
 Position of fore feet in action, 79.
 Rash horse, advice on riding, 18 *seq.*
 "Refusing," 65.
 Sensitive and highly-strung, 3.
 "Slug," management required by, 24.
 Wall-jumping, 132.
 Yearling, 158.
 Young, apt to swerve, 74.
 Young horse in bog, 3.
 (*See* also Irish Hunters and Thorough-bred Horses.)
Horse-breakers not varying their system, 45.
Horsemanship—
 Art of, 53.
 Every rider his own system, 80.
 First principles of, 70.
 Qualities necessary for, 1, 2, 11, 12, 13, 239, 240.

Horsewoman, style adopted by, 72.
Howcott, Mark, whip, 201.
Hunter, qualities for perfect, 31.
Hunters not really fond of jumping, 187.
Hunting—
 Advice on start on hack, 121 *seq.*
 Fields to be avoided, 134.
 Second horses introduced, 38.
Hunting-field—
 As school for cavalry officers, 178.
 As school for leaping, 14.
 "What kills is the pace," 156.
Hunting in provinces and shires, 219–224, 225, *seq.*
"Hunting parsons," 82.
Hunting pictures of Leicestershire and Northamptonshire, 36.

I

Ireland, fences in, 137.
Ireland, no cart-horse blood till recently, 154.
Irish horse-breaking, 142.
Irish hunters, 137 *seq.*
 Accoutrements, 144.
 At stone-gap, 145.
 Difficulty of buying, 152.
 Experience needful in judging, 151.
 Go shortest way, 149.
 In shires, 147, 148.
 Jumping 146 ;
  "at short notice," 149.
 Objection to, 152, 153.
 Style of jumping, 137, 139.
 System for training "an accomplished lepper," 15.
 Timber-jumping, 147.
 "Training," 140, 142.
 Well-bred, 153.
Irishmen, natural insight into character of horse, 142.
Irishmen ride with light bridle, 73, 139.

245

INDEX

J

Jersey, Lord, on Shuttlecock's disinclination to jump, 161, 162.
Jersey, Lord, riding at timber, 23.
"John Gilpin" quoted, 71.
Johnston, Sir Frederic, not using spurs, 62.
"Jorrocks" as hard rider, 125.
"Jorrocks" on seat, 89.
Judicious coercion, 15.
Jumping, advice on, 75, 78.
Jumping timber, 22; examples of different methods, 22, 23.
Juvenal, metaphor from horses, 154.

K

"King of the Golden Mines," 228.
Kingsley, Charles, "Knight's Last Leap at Alten-ahr" quoted, 68.
Knight, stag-hunting on Exmoor, 199.
Knightley, Sir Charles, training "Sir Marinel," 160.

L

Ladies in hunting-field, advice to, 117, 118.
Ladies' pluck in riding, example of, 115.
Ladies using spur, 60.
Lawrenson, General, horsemanship, 51, 86.
Leg-power, use of, in riding, 72.
Liverpool, pace and distance of the, 158.
Lovell, of New Forest, horsemanship, 17.
Lovell, invention for bridoon, 39.
Lowther, Hugh, not using spurs, 62.

M

Man's supremacy over beasts, reason of, 16.

"Mars," Lord Cardigan's hunter, 111.
Martingale unknown to Greeks, 35.
Mason, Jem—
Instructions to beginner, 73.
Using spurs, 64.
Warning to Lord Strathmore, 106.
Matthew's tactics, 214, 219.
Maxse, fineness of hand, 32.
Mayo, Lord—
Horse ridden with Pytchley, 169.
Horsemanship, 129.
Story of Irish attendant, 130.
Mechanical horse in Piccadilly, account of, 93 seq.
Melton-Spinney, 148.
Hounds killing by moonlight in, 235.
Melton Steeplechase (1864), 84.
Melton, weighing hunters at, 168.
Mesmer, disciples of, 16.
Mexican spurs, 67.
Middleham Moor, 156.
Miles, Colonel, jumping six-foot fence, 132.
Morgan, Ben, story of, 9.

N

Nerve and pluck, 104, 107.
Newmarket Heath, 156.
Nimrod on horses' strength, 167.
Nose-band, author's prejudice against, 19.

O

Oriental cavalry soldier, position in saddle, 90.

P

Payne, Charles, on "natural death" of foxes, 189.
Pearson, General, charging timber, 22.
Pelham bridle unpopular in England, 42.

INDEX

Plato, 99.
Pluck and nerve, 104, 107.
Portman, stag-hunting, 208.
Portman, with fox-hounds, 184.
Powell riding over high timber, 111.
Presence of mind necessary for riding, 11.
Provinces, 210 *seq.*
Pytchley, finest hunting country in England, 236.

Q

Quorn, 236.
Fences, 225.
Hounds, 211, 212

R

Ranksborough, coming from, 148, 157.
Rarey and judicious coercion, 15.
Reins, long, advantages of, 73.
Reins, loose, question of, 50.
Rider, rule for position of, 97, 100.
Riding—
Attitudes adopted in, 90.
Round corners, advice on, 85.
Two-handed, 74.
Rothschild, Baron, hunting-bridge over Rowsham, 188.
Rothschild, Baron, stag-hounds, 195.
Rothschild, Leopold, hunting carted deer, 201.
Rothschild, Sir Nathaniel, hunting carted deer, 200, 201.
Rotten Row, riding in, 85.
Rowsham forded by bullocks, 188.
Russell, Rev. John, stag-hunting, 197.

S

Saddle, open or plain-flapped, 96.
Facility for moving leg in, 97.
Saddles, padded *versus* open, 96 *seq.*

Seat, 89 *seq.*
How to obtain firm, 101.
Strong, 101.
Shires, 225 *seq.*
Run in, 227 *seq.*
Shuttlecock, Billesdon Coplow poem quoted on, 161.
" Sir Marinel," Sir Charles Knightley's hunter, 160.
Smith, Assheton—
Diagonal jump, 126.
On knowing how to fall, 238.
Riding at timber, 23.
Style of riding, 107.
Smith, Captain Arthur, horsemanship, 108.
Smith, Captain Arthur, riding at timber, 22.
Smith, Tom, skill and daring of, 108.
Snaffle, 34.
Somerset, Granville, stag-hunting, 197, 199.
Spencer, Lord, as Master of the Pytchley, 236.
Spencer, Lord, horsemanship, 6.
Sportswomen, 116, 117.
Spur—
Abuse of, 56 *seq.*
For hack, 59.
In riding-schools, 57.
Inconvenient when rider is down, 66.
Why used in hunting-field, 62, 63.
Stag-hounds, riding *at*, 193 *seq.*
" Combes," 197.
Hounds to have plenty of room, 204.
No fixed rules for, 193.
On Exmoor, 195.
" Riding the deer," 204.
Running compared with foxhounds, 196.
" Tufting," 199.
Steeplechase riders' fine hands, 83.
Stirrup, length of, 91.
Stone-gap, Ireland, 145.
Stour, River, good friend to deer, 208.
Strathmore, Lord, 106.

INDEX